"Maggie's triumphant story o
actualization in corporate Ar
common role as an Executive Assistant will convince
anyone about the power of belief. Maggie's deep-seated
belief that she is not only worthy of more, but deserving
as well, has transformed her life from being a likely high
school drop-out without direction, to a CEO's Right Hand.
Harnessing this power of belief coupled with the relentless
will to execute flawlessly as an unrepenting generalist
makes her story an inspiration for anyone curious about
how it is possible to have it all, while perceived by the
world as being "just an admin"."

-Al-Husein Madhany
Life Coach & Co-Founder of ELS Talent Advisors

"If it were not for Maggie Jacobs, I would not be on
LinkedIn, amongst many other career enhancing decisions
which Maggie confidently guided me towards when I was
building my business. Meeting Maggie was divine timing
for where I was at that time in my life, and I continue to
learn from her every single time we talk. In this beautiful
book, Maggie has the courage to tell her whole story, and
in the process, inspires all of us to live a more authentic
life, while following our dreams. A must read!"

-Libby Moore, Executive Coach,
Speaker, & former Chief of Staff to Oprah Winfrey

"If you're ok with the status quo, don't read this book. But,
if you're ready to reclaim control of your career and become
an elevated assistant, Maggie's book is a must read."

-Jeremy Burrows, Founder of LeaderAssistant.com
and AssistantsGuide.com,
Host of The Leader Assistant Podcast

"Rarely do I run into someone whom I immediately feel some sense of kinship with. When I met Maggie for the first time several years ago, I intrinsically knew she was special and destined for big things. Fast forward to now and I'm filled with immense pride knowing that she has discovered her power and become a force. Upon reading Maggie's book, I finally got a lot of the context that was missing in our previous meetings and conversations. The revelations in this book speak volumes to the woman Maggie has become, the voice she's found, and the honesty and integrity with which she operates.

The stories within the book are equal parts autobiographical and a call to action for EAs looking to elevate themselves and their careers. There's no perfect blueprint to get to the top. Everyone has a history that influences their outcomes. What Maggie beautifully represents in this book is the power of self-forgiveness, finding direction and belief, obeying your intuition, and opening your damn mouth and actually asking for what you want. I love this book because it's real, incredibly honest, and a fantastic account of a life once plagued with challenges and disappointment now filled with wonder, confidence, and intention. It's an honor to know that my words had such a positive impact on Maggie. This book will do exactly the same for the masses who read it. Especially the passionate ones."

-Phoenix Normand
Chief at trīb + BounceBack,
Author of AS I SEE IT Volume 1: Business

The Elevated EA

FIND YOUR VOICE & OWN YOUR FUTURE AS AN EXECUTIVE ASSISTANT

MAGGIE JACOBS

For information, contact
Foresight Book Publishing
Chattanooga, TN 37419

FORESIGHT BOOK PUBLISHING
ForesightPublishingNow.com
Info@ForesightPublishingNow.com

Dedication

To Mom and Dad for giving me life and for being the parents you were and are—so I could be the person I am today.

To Grandma and Kitty for loving me unconditionally as your own and instilling in me the values that matter most in life: integrity, kindness, humor, love, and grace.

To my many teachers—family, friends, colleagues past and present, communities and groups who welcome, support, and love me—and to everyone with whom I've interacted.

Lastly, to my foundation, my rock, my husband, Scott: thank you for joining me on this journey.

Table of Contents

Foreword

Over the past 23 years, I've had the opportunity to help establish and lead several organizations to success. Throughout my early career, I'd always inherited an executive assistant and found myself jealous of other executives who seemingly had a different kind of relationship with their EA. While others had longstanding partnerships, based on years of working together, my experience with EAs had always been more transactional, focused on managing things like travel, calendaring, and expenses.

Perhaps I just didn't ask for the right things or spend enough time with my EA to really gel the relationship. Or maybe, I thought, it just takes years of working together to develop the kind of symbiotic relationship I saw with other executives and their EAs. Or, maybe I just hadn't gotten lucky enough to be assigned the right person for me.

In any case, I always figured I could use all the help I could get, and I appreciated the hard work that goes into the job. Plus, I used to think I didn't really need that much help. I'd be thrilled to get a little assistance with travel plans, keeping me out of time-wasting meetings, or helping me prepare for a presentation.

It wasn't until I came to 6sense and met Maggie that I realized what was possible.

As CEO, I'm responsible for advancing the company's vision, setting the tone and culture, and directing the operations of the business. And like most CEOs, I have what I consider to be an outstanding executive leadership team who help me to guide and direct the business. But as great as my team is, no single individual sees more, or shares more of the challenges of what it means to be CEO than my EA, Maggie.

My relationship with Maggie has changed my view of not only the role an EA can play in supporting an executive, but in supporting the business.

Maggie is a true partner in productivity and together we actively collaborate on management efficiency, creating high performing teams, driving corporate culture, and more. Maggie actively looks for opportunities within the company and for myself for growth and development, and together we plan and execute against our goals. She pushes me every single day to bring my "A" game, my best self.

But this didn't happen by accident or overnight. Getting here took a commitment from both of us.

For my part, I had to be willing to expose a certain amount of weakness, vulnerability. I had to admit I didn't have every answer, I didn't see everything. For many CEOs, and for me especially, this level of trust was not something easily given, but Maggie did her part to earn it.

Maggie regularly attends leadership meetings, sits in on my key 1:1s, helps facilitate town halls, and assists with corporate communications to understand how the business operates. She asks questions and digests learnings in order to grow her understanding of the challenges we face as an organization, and is able to anticipate where, when and how I operate keeping me aligned both strategically and tactically.

I love that she cares enough about me, the company, and our mission to push us to engage at a higher level. Part taskmaster, part confidant, part advisor, and part friend, Maggie has become an invaluable member of my team in ways I never imagined possible from an EA.

I believe this book presents a unique and compelling opportunity for EAs and executives alike to rethink what's possible from the role. As an EA, you are in a remarkable position to impact the business in ways others in the organization simply can't. I encourage you to read this book and leverage Maggie's insights to rethink what's possible, and to build a different kind of relationship with your executive based on collaboration, shared goals, and trust.

But in order to do that, you'll need to elevate your game.

Jason Zintak, President & CEO of 6sense

This is the true joy in life, the being used for a purpose recognized by yourself as a mighty one; the being a force of nature instead of a feverish, selfish little clod of ailments and grievances complaining that the world will not devote itself to making you happy.

–George Bernard Shaw

Acknowledgments

I'd like to acknowledge Melissa Toboni for giving me exactly what I needed when I needed it; Bonnie Low-Kramen for seeing something in me I couldn't see in myself; Vickie Sokol Evans for teaching me my Microsoft technical chops that have seven-figure ROI, in time and dollars saved across the organization; Jean Francese for instilling in me the confidence to ask for and receive my first six figures; Lorna Koep for your gentle guidance and patient persistence; Jan Jones for writing a book that spoke to executives to articulate the impact we make and value we provide; Dasha Vasilyeva for planting seeds early and often—I see you!

Pablo Pollard for being my first executive "soul mate"—I only wish I'd seen it sooner; Ivanna Ivanitska for being a shining example of what's possible with hunger and commitment. You're the best student and champion anyone could ask for; Jorah Ryken for many things, particularly getting through to me so I would keep my mouth shut when it mattered most; Cheryl Pierce for your steady, patient encouragement and for opening the doors to something I never thought possible. You're my Tony Robbins, soul sister; Tony Robbins for giving me permission to own my story and for showing me that life is happening for me not to me; Al-Husein Madhany for your unwavering commitment to my success, despite my natural resistance and occasional stubbornness; Phoenix Normand for being unapologetically you and providing a framework for powerful conversations; Jeremy Burrows for sharing your experience and insight and giving so

much to our community; Libby Moore, you are a remarkable, phenomenal, and sensational human being, and I'm grateful for the strength and courage you've given me over the years; Joyce Gidel, you are truly a miracle worker; Avani Shahlenis for your guidance and coaching and for showing me my ridiculous expectations and timelines; Claudia Laughter for consistently expecting more from me—I hear you; Veronica Karas for showing me what it means to really burn the boats. You inspire me; Jolynn Swafford for your infinite wisdom; Dale Chube for your expertise and our accountability calls—This is really happening!; Lauren Hasson for not allowing my resistance to win in writing this book; MG FTW+! Thank you for graciously answering my endless questions. I appreciate you, your insight, and your sense of humor so much!; Jason Zintak for your patience, generosity, and unknowingly enabling me to become the person I am today. Our partnership is one I wish all EAs could experience for themselves in their careers.

I'd also like to acknowledge my husband, Scott Jacobs, for being my biggest fan, for loving me unconditionally, and for saying, "Don't worry about spending time with me. I will not be the reason you do not write this book." Thank you for constantly encouraging and gently pushing me when I wanted to give up so many times. I love you.

With the utmost appreciation and gratitude, thank you.

Maggie

Introduction

Becoming an executive assistant was my fallback plan. It was a temporary strategy designed to allow me to remain invisible and exist in a world where I could hide in plain sight, play small, fly under the radar, and work behind the scenes. Life wouldn't be asking too much of me, and that was fine by me.

But a lot has changed since then. Today, I work alongside the CEO of a successful tech company, I lead trainings, coach clients, and I occasionally speak at EA conferences. I've been tapped for roles supporting C-level executives, I've turned down interview opportunities at Big Name companies, and I've said "No Thanks" to a six-figure Deputy Chief of Staff position. I've been a guest on EA webinars and podcasts, and I am friendly with several tech, motivational, and EA legends and influencers around the globe.

I share all of this hesitantly and with humility and awe as I pause and reflect on how far I've come. But I'm proud to say that I am now in a position that affords me the freedom, flexibility, and autonomy to live a life that suits me well, and that is fulfilling, committed to service, and a contribution to others.

So, how the hell did I get here?

If someone had asked me, "Where do you see yourself at the age of 33?" when I was a kid or a teen, I would have replied matter-of-factly: "Dead."

I didn't get where I am by virtue of a straight line. I've lied and cheated. I've been written up, suspended, and expelled. I've been fired.

I've partied my ass off so bad that blackouts were my norm. I've been addicted to drugs and alcohol, and I've said and done hurtful things. I've been through trials and trauma, betrayal and blame, bitterness and resentment. I survived an empty, lonely childhood when I thought the world owed me something.

My attitude was bad, even as a child. When I was 12 years old, a therapist told my mother that my attitude was callous, apathetic, and angry. "It's unlikely she'll go to college or even finish high school," she concluded.

"What's wrong with me?" I asked myself incessantly. "I'm not good enough. I don't care. What's the point?" These questions hammered in my mind. Along with: "Fuck this. Fuck you. Fuck it." The chorus of negativity swelled with emotion and hurt in my mind. And it set the foundation for my behavior for the first 28 years of my life.

And yet, these days, other people are asking me a very different set of questions: "How did you get to where you are? What did you do? What steps did you take?" This line of questioning confused me at first. I never thought of myself as someone others would want to emulate or as someone having skills that others would want to learn from. My life has been messy and tumultuous. The success I enjoy now certainly didn't happen overnight. To be honest, the fact that I am where I am today is nothing short of a miracle—a miracle fueled by sheer grit and sustained by determination. I'm not famous, I don't have awards or accolades or other symbols of success, but I am living a life beyond what I could have ever hoped for. And that certainly is a miracle for someone who never had a vision, a direction, or even any dreams to speak of.

So, no, I didn't just slip on a banana peel and get to be the way I am today. Once I realized my life wasn't going to turn around on its own, I dug in, dug deep, and devoted myself to the relentless pursuit of training and development. I realized I had to clean up my act and re-engineer myself within the world I live in. To do so, I had to face decades of pain, fear, shame, guilt and denial. I had to walk through the traumas and abandonment, step up to find my voice, and live a life worth living. I had to get complete with my past and live life from a place of acceptance and forgiveness (of myself and others)—a life beyond my wildest dreams.

So, I don't really have a master plan or a list of steps to offer anyone to follow in my footsteps. (Anyway, you really wouldn't want to follow in my footsteps!) This isn't a "How To" guide for you to scale your professional ladder and go from zero to hero in the time it takes to read this book. And it's certainly not a one-size-fits-all recipe for a successful, pain-free, happy life.

But I do have some incredible insights and lessons that have kept me on target, energized my efforts, and empowered me to step up higher than I ever thought possible. I've discovered that there are specific principles and ways of being that, if applied consistently, over time, will dramatically increase your chance of a living a life you love. If only I'd been exposed to them the first 33 years of my life...

I've been coached and guided by some of the most powerful thought leaders around who have inspired me to no end and helped me change the trajectory of my life. Without them, I couldn't have gotten to where I am today. That's why, even more than my personal story, I want to share with you many of the attitudes and tools that have opened doors for me and the ideas that have opened my own mind to what's possible for me. I want to share with you how to believe in yourself and invest in yourself. How to see your job, yourself, your salary, and your boss in a new light that empowers and ignites you. I want to give you some new ideas about how to get through your day-to-day challenges and begin to create a vibrant network and a sense of belonging that supports your own wildest dreams. I want to help you elevate your own vision of who you want to become—as an EA and beyond.

I'm here to tell you the truth, because I've been through hell and back, and I know what's possible. You *can* exceed your own expectations. You *do* deserve it. You *are* worth it. And you can do it!

1

FAST TRACK TO NOWHERE

Life did not get handed to me on a silver platter. Born in the Bay Area, I was only two years old when I was molested by a family member. When it happened for the second time, I had the presence of mind to tell my babysitter, and she told my parents. My mother believed me. My father, on the other hand, was adamant that nothing had really happened. And in the next few weeks, he was able to produce a sworn affidavit saying as much. But it was ludicrous, of course. It was not a rape case; there weren't any telltale fluids to test for. How could they come up with any evidence and determine that something did not happen?

So my mom decided that she wanted to remove me from the environment altogether and elected to move the two of us to the Bay Area to start life over together. Of course, I was too young to understand what was happening and why. I tried to make sense of it, but no one explained any of it to me. I just felt like I had been yanked away from the rest of our family. I felt like my dad had abandoned me and I didn't know why. Then, the incomprehensible distance between us and the rest of the family deepened my wounds; I would no longer be able to spend time with that whole side of our family, including my dad and my half-sister. A whole slice of my life had been pulled away from me. My insides felt split apart, and there was nothing I could do about it.

The move itself was confusing and shocking to me, and I had no idea why my world had to be disrupted so badly. The only way I could make sense of it was to think that there must be something wrong with *me*. After all, the other kids I knew seemed "normal." They seemed to have siblings and dads and families. But I had no siblings, no dad, no family, really. I didn't have other things that the other kids seemed to have, too. I got hand-me-downs when everyone else seemed to be sporting new clothes. I had no rollerblades. I didn't play sports or participate in those kinds of activities when I was growing up. Didn't attend camp, didn't go skiing, didn't do most things that seemingly "normal" kids do. And, not having those experiences, I never really learned to socialize in any meaningful way, either. Instead, I learned to fend for myself. I felt way too different from everybody else to be comfortable. I figured I was a loser. I didn't matter. They didn't love me. Feeling unworthy and unlovable was my baseline.

My mother, having been suddenly thrown into the role of being a single mom, had some challenges with the job. She had grown up with an alcoholic father herself, so maybe that robbed her of healthy parenting skills. It might have affected her in a way that I wouldn't be able to understand for many, many years. Whatever the reason, my mother seemed to eschew motherhood. She made a habit of not spending much time with me; she couldn't sit still long enough to stay at home with me. She set me up with a new babysitter time and time again; she always seemed to be dumping me in one house or another whenever she could. Love? What's that?

Even when she was in the same room as me, my mom didn't show up as present to me. Making matters worse, although she was well-educated with two master's and half a doctorate to her name, she couldn't seem to be able to hold down a job. My environment felt chaotic, uncertain, and confusing, and I can't say it did much for my self-esteem.

Not surprisingly, my attitude started to go south even at a young age. As I got a little older, I got more brazen and rebellious.

I wasn't comfortable in my own skin, and it showed. School wasn't much fun, either. I was small in size, so I was an easy target to bullies. I was different, too, and it showed.

At the age of six, I woke up one morning to learn that my mom had been in a car accident the night before. She was lying in bed with ice packs and braces and that sort of thing. She told everyone that it was a "closed head injury," but I also understood that she was known for being something of a hypochondriac. I never quite knew if it was real or not. But I have to admit that, ever since then, she hasn't been able to perform some tasks at the expected level. None of it was ever spelled out for me.

So, at six years old, I realized I needed to grow up fast. I vividly remember her having a hard time just trying to lift a gallon of milk. And there I was, a puny kid, schlepping milk, carrying grocery bags from the car, putting groceries away, and cooking for her. After all, it was just the two of us—and one of us wasn't doing much.

Since I was way too young to drive, I rode my bicycle to the grocery store on weekends, picked up the food I thought we'd need for the week, and rode back home. I carried what I could with me on the bike. Of course, every once in a while, despite my best intentions, I'd inevitably drop the gallon of milk before I got it to my bike, and all I could do was watch helplessly as the plastic fell and shattered everywhere. It didn't take me long to learn how to become an expert in instant pasta and ramen and peanut butter and jelly sandwiches. I became a master at boiling water.

The first time I tried to make a purchase at the deli counter at the grocery store by myself was a total bust. I was about seven, not even tall enough to see over the counter, much less be seen by the clerk. I finally flagged someone down to talk to me, hoping they'd treat me like an adult and help me with my deli needs for the day.

"Smoked turkey, please," I said cheerfully.

"Sure thing, sweetheart. Where's your mother?"

"She's at home in bed," I replied.

That didn't go over well. In a condescending tone, she informed me that I needed to have a parent with me to order from the deli.

I'm not sure who was more shocked, the clerk, having to answer to a seven-year-old, or me, leaving the grocery store without my turkey. But worse, seeds of bitterness, anger, and resentment started to get planted in my heart. It was more than just going home without a certain deli cut; if I couldn't bring home some turkey, it meant I'd have to go another week of making packaged pasta or ramen and visiting friends in the neighborhood to swing a hot meal. (I had gotten good at convincing neighbors to feed me from time to time.) To my young mind, it was all more evidence that something was wrong with me.

But the following weekend, I was pleasantly surprised when my mom was up for the trip to the grocery store. It was my chance. After the two of us made our rounds through the store, we approached the deli counter. I was determined to never have to leave that counter again without my turkey, so I watched, listened, and learned.

"Half a pound of smoked turkey, thinly sliced, please," my mom said to the clerk. Within a few minutes, the clerk handed over the soft pile of meat, and we were on our way.

A few weeks later, I was back at the deli counter, alone.

"Smoked turkey, please. Half a pound, thinly sliced," I said confidently.

"Sure dear. Where's your mother?"

I almost blurted out the truth: "At home, in bed," but something else came out instead.

"She's shopping in another aisle," I smiled genially.

"Well, okay, hon. Give me a few minutes. I'll have it right up for you."

I beamed. It worked!

My life circumstances were forcing me to learn how to provide for myself, whether I liked it or not. There wasn't any time to stop and smell the roses or to just enjoy life. I had to do everything I could to make sure that I had everything I needed and that my mom had everything she needed to function. I learned the art of being fiercely independent and never having to rely on anyone. It was my strength. Whatever I had to do, I figured there must be a way that I could do it even better. I became incredibly focused on efficiency and effectiveness.

Of course, if I wanted something done, I'd have to do it myself. I couldn't rely on anyone else, and I had to figure things out on my own. I had to make things happen. After all, who else was going to do it? I let my mom know that I didn't need her. "I got this," I told myself, whatever "this" was. I was just fine taking care of myself, I told everyone, including myself. I didn't want anyone's help.

Not surprisingly, I started getting into trouble at an early age. By second grade, I was misbehaving in school, being a little too disruptive, a little too loud. At the same time, the school had generously bestowed upon me the label, "Talented and Gifted" (TAG), but it only added to my distress. They'd pull out all the TAG kids from class a couple times a week and put them into smaller group settings to study together. But whenever I returned to class, my classmates teased me. "Where were you?" they taunted. "What were you doing, dork?" As kids can be—they were cruel. I felt more like an outsider than ever. I quickly learned that if I ignored a school assignment or two, the invites to the TAG program would stop coming and the teasing would stop, too.

But when I stopped participating in TAG, I got more rebellious in class. I'd make obnoxious comments, call out answers, and do anything to get attention—positive or negative. I earned some new labels, like "class clown" and "disruptive," but I didn't care. "Fuck you" was my attitude. The more they thought I was a bad kid, the more I acted out. It was my new normal.

Now, if you've ever spent much time in the principal's office, you know you have a lot of downtime—and for me, it was time to watch, listen, and absorb. I was mesmerized by how the office ladies answered the phones, how they greeted visitors so cheerfully, how they seemed to handle every request with finesse—from demanding parents to tantrum-throwing kids. "Good morning, Greenway Elementary! How many I direct your call?" They ran a seamless shop, and I was entranced by it. I soaked it all in. In fact, I was there so much that they eventually put me to work stapling, folding, stuffing, and sealing envelopes. Looking back, I think I was actually a good kid—I was just yearning for attention and didn't know how to ask for it.

Still, my negative thinking deepened. What used to be, "They don't love me," turned into, "I don't need them anyway. Screw them." I started pushing people away, building nearly impenetrable, indestructible walls around myself. I wasn't going to let anyone in because I didn't want to be hurt or abandoned again. I was acting out.

And then another friend of the family tried to molest me.

When I was 12, my mom took me for a psych evaluation. "Maggie has a 'fuck you' attitude," the therapist said. "On her current path, she won't attend college and it's highly unlikely she'll finish high school." Lovely, I thought. There's no hope for me. That prediction became the new lens through which I viewed myself, my world, and my place in it. No hope. No point. Screw you. My negative thinking would spiral downward for many years and ended up impacting my personal and professional relationships for many years to come.

It was time to move again when I was 13. My mom decided to move us to Trout Lake, Washington, 85 miles north of Portland, Oregon, population 1,000. The people who lived in Trout Lake tended to be very religious and generally married their high school sweethearts, bought a house, and remained in town to live. The school was a very good, very small, K-12 school with only 173 kids. It was quite hands-on.

By that time, I had grown to 5'8" and looked like I was 20. I was an oddball. I must have been putting out a different vibe, too, because people seemed to be naturally drawn to me to get help with things, answer questions, or point them in the right direction. When I walked into art class on my first day of eighth grade, for example, the teacher looked at me and asked, "Are you my senior TA?" I shook my head and quietly took my seat.

The move to Trout Lake was something of a boon for me since it gave me a fresh start, and I was in desperate need of it. I was at a new school, in a class of only 13, and I didn't have the reputation of being a troublemaker to prejudice everyone I came into contact with.

While my mom had valiantly removed me from a toxic environment and had set up the two of us plus my grandmother in a new home in a new town, she still had some trouble fulfilling the usual responsibilities of motherhood. She had difficulties providing for us and relied heavily on the people she knew to get by. She borrowed money from family and friends and then didn't seem to be able to handle what she had very well, either. She'd frequently be out with the boyfriend she had at the time, without giving any of us an explanation.

Now when I look back, I consider growing up with my mom both a blessing and a curse. While she had taken me away from everything I knew as my family and raised me on her own, with no siblings and no father, the blessing was that I decided with every fiber of my being that I would do everything I could to not end up like her. To paraphrase Tony Robbins: if my mom had been the mother I wanted her to be, I wouldn't be the person I am today. So, there you go.

The walls that protect you also imprison you.

Thankfully, my grandmother had moved in with us and she was around at the time to help parent and guide me as best she could. She taught me about some of the most important principles of life—things like integrity, generosity, and compassion—principles I orient my life around today. But it would take me quite a few more years, and the earth-shattering jolt of hitting rock bottom, before I would ever learn to do that.

***

I soon took a job at a pizza-and-burger joint called, "Time Out Pizza n' More." I started there as a waitress, then became a server, and after a few months, I eventually became a cook. The owner trusted me so much that on the weekends, when business was slow, she'd leave me to run the shop while she'd take off to go grocery shopping. I'd be the only one there to manage things. I took orders, did the cooking, and watched over anything else that was needed. I felt good about what I thought I could do and how well I could perform the tasks that were given to me.

Yes, I was able to take on responsibility. I knew myself to be quite capable of being efficient and productive. But I still had no idea what "boundaries" were. I didn't have a voice of my own. I was despondent and indifferent, and I didn't really care what happened to me. I was just putting one foot in front of the other, trying to survive.

***

Without a mother present enough to teach me the social ropes, and having felt like damaged goods for so long, my social life was pretty much nonexistent. So I filled that void by making friends with the women in that school office. Sometimes I'd visit by choice—not just by punishment. At lunchtime, instead of hanging out with the kids in their cliques, I made myself useful in the office. I was good at the tasks they gave me and they welcomed my help. It felt good to actually contribute something of value during my break periods.

For my last two years in high school, we decided to make it official, and I signed on as a Teacher's Assistant. But my poor attitude was still running the show. I was partying by then—smoking pot and drinking and being as lazy as I could get away with. Since I could do so well in school without hardly trying, I wondered why I should bother working hard at all.

Just before my senior year of school, my grandmother's health started to decline precipitously. She wanted to move back to California's Bay Area to be around the rest of the family—and I wanted to go with her. My mom didn't like it, but she knew she couldn't stop me, so I moved to California with my grandmother. But I didn't end up living with her. Grandma moved back in with my grandfather in Los Altos, and I moved in with an aunt and uncle in Scotts Valley, a small town near Santa Cruz.

Scotts Valley High was a brand new school. The class size was about 120, so, while still being small, it was ten times as big as my last school. I didn't know anyone, so once again, I was blessed with a fresh start. And I dug in. I figured out a way to tailor my schedule so I could be a full-time student but still work 25 to 40 hours a week as a checker at a grocery store and earn some money. My schedule left little time for recreational activities and I had very few friends, so I became a stellar student. Even with my half-ass attitude over the previous few years, I worked my butt off and was able to graduate with a 3.8 average.

But what was I going to do *after* high school?

I am who I've been looking for.
–Adam Roa

When people suggested to me that I should continue my education after high school, college wasn't even on my radar. I didn't know anything about education. I didn't have a vision for myself, I had no goals, no direction. I was just showing up day to day. And so, when it came time to apply for schools, I thought, okay, I'll just apply to a couple based on what people recommend. One of my aunts happened to mention that California State University at Chico was beautiful and that a friend of hers had a daughter who went there. So I applied. And when I received my acceptance letter, the choice was made for me. Unfortunately, no one warned me that Chico had once been ranked the number one party school in the country by Playboy Magazine.

To be clear: any school can be a party school; it's about what you make of it. From the choices you make to the friends you surround yourself with, your outcome is largely determined by you. But having a full year behind me as a working professional and a stellar high school student turned out to be my saving grace as I headed into college.

Once I got to Chico, I immediately signed myself up for 8:00 a.m. classes every single day of the week. I literally didn't know you could make other choices. So, three days a week, I'd be finished with school by 10 a.m.—and I thought I was a genius. Now, being finished by 10 a.m. probably sounds like a great idea to a lot of people—especially those who don't have addictive personalities like I do. But I had gotten so used to showing up for my 7:40 a.m. classes in high school, it didn't even occur to me I could start the day later in college.

For the first few semesters at Chico, I applied myself to my schoolwork, and I crushed it academically. My grades were great. But after about a year and half, I realized that I had created such a great foundation for a good grade average that I would be able to coast through the rest of my time in school. It was an incredibly solid foundation of work that let me do little more than party for the remainder of my college career.

So, as I came of legal drinking age, the partying magnified. I literally designed my schedule around the cheapest happy hours at the local bars. Of course, as I partied more, my attendance in class dwindled. During my first semester, I had limited my partying to just the weekends, but as I became more comfortable with my surroundings, I became more social and made a habit of making exceptions to my "weekends-only" rule. After all, Thursday nights were "almost" the weekend—right?

> *All suffering is about obsession of self.*
> *Expect less, appreciate more.*
> *–Tony Robbins*

One day, I was sitting in class, reeking of booze from the night before, but ballsy enough to raise my hand to answer a question. Seeing my raised hand, the professor pleaded with the rest of the class:

"Come on, you guys. Maggie thinks her weekends start on *Thursdays*, and *she's* participating. Why can't the rest of you show up?"

I didn't think I had a problem at the time. But hearing someone else—particularly a person of authority—point it out made me reconsider.

When I arrived at Chico, I selected political science as a major. Looking back, I'm not really sure what I would have done with it. I think at some point I wanted to be a cop. A couple semesters in, I changed my major to nutrition when I started to develop an appreciation for the fiber content of food products on nutrition labels. But once it dawned on me how much biology and science would be required of me to pursue a passion for nutrition, I decided I wanted to choose something that would be easier on me. I wanted to find an area that I could do reasonably well in—or at least not fail. In the meantime, I filled my days by numbing and escaping from whatever it was in my past that was making me miserable.

Even with my ceaseless partying, I graduated with a degree in Business Administration and Management in 2007. I spent the next six years largely in a downward spiral of partying, negativity, hopelessness, reactivity, numbness, depression, black-outs, self-hatred, and more partying.

Nothing changed until 2013. Except that I got myself a job that taught me about who I did—and didn't—want to be.

2
CRASH AND BURN

When I was still a junior at Chico, I needed to choose an elective, a course that draws you personally but that fulfills a general education requirement at the same time, like ecology, art, or political science. The topic of financial literacy intrigued me. It sounded practical and possibly valuable, so I chose it as my elective. The class turned out to be pretty interesting, in spite of my general resistance to getting too serious about anything.

A Little Direction

One of the class requirements was to read Suze Orman's book, *The Money Book for the Young, Fabulous & Broke,* which gave really clear step-by-step advice about managing money, credit scores, career moves, and more for the young. The book thoroughly energized and inspired me. When I looked around me at the kids in my class, and thought about all the students on campus, it seemed that everything Orman talked about should probably be required reading no matter what people were studying. So many students didn't even know how to balance a checkbook and weren't getting warned not to sign up for the credit cards with ridiculously high interest rates that were scattered across campus. It felt like a farce that people would go to school, sign up for a bunch of credit cards, and then graduate with a load of debt.

Then a unique thought planted itself in my mind: *I want to stop this. I want to be a force for good!* With a degree in Business Administration and Entrepreneurship under my belt, I was inspired to teach people financial literacy—something most of us didn't learn in school, yet it applies to everyone in society today. I was feeling compelled to help other people; I wanted to help them prioritize and dominate their financial future, and even realize their dreams. Even though I was wasted half of my waking hours, I decided that I wanted to get licensed and become a financial advisor. I was on to something. I just *knew* I was going to change *the world!*

Finally, I had some sort of direction! Finally, I was off to the races. I studied for and obtained my Series 6, 63, and insurance licenses, which gave me what I thought I needed to start my career to bring financial health to the world. Then, I got a job as a financial advisor at AIG Wealth Advisors.

Unfortunately, it didn't go well.

It was 2008, and the market was crashing fast all around us. Nobody wanted to hand their money over to a 22-year-old to manage at a time when all of the financial structures around us looked doomed to implode. On top of that, the role I had signed up for was 100% commission-based, and worse yet, its strategy for drumming up new business was based on the "start with your friends and family" model. The job was not a good fit for me, to put it mildly. I was destined to fail. I was completely unprepared for what the job would require—I didn't understand sales at all, and I didn't realize that money can be such an emotional topic. You had to talk to people about their feelings sometimes more than you talk to them about numbers.

After nearly a year of advising, I threw in the towel. But what was I going to do or be? What did I do well? I was still a raging alcoholic. No one sent me the memo that said that once you graduate, you don't drink and party like you did in college. I was still going at it big time. Blackouts were the norm for me. If someone had told me that most people actually graduate from partying hearty at college, I was too wasted to hear it.

I felt trapped. I felt like a failure because I couldn't hack it as a financial advisor. And because the drinking had taken over my life. Still, I didn't necessarily *know* that I had a problem. My grandfather had been an alcoholic, and he always drank alone, so I figured that an alcoholic was a person who drinks alone. I didn't party alone, so I must not be an alcoholic or a drug addict, right? Hardly. I wasn't able to socialize without liquid encouragement. I was terribly uncomfortable in my own skin, and I was numbing myself with altering substances. After I graduated and moved to San Francisco, I would go to gay nightclubs because they were safe for me as a female. And I could get as fucked up as I wanted and not have to worry about who was trying to get in my pants. It was a win-win.

My altered states of drugs and alcohol fueled my emotional turmoil and engaged my whole mental labyrinth of disempowering thoughts, beliefs, and questions. *Why me? Who cares? What's the point? What's wrong with me? Why is this happening to me? What did I do to deserve this? I will surely never amount to anything. Life isn't fair. This would be much easier if I were dead.* And on and on.

The writing was on the wall. I knew I had to do something other than be a financial advisor if I was going to survive in any way. With the economy melting down, and a prevailing feeling of scarcity and fear everywhere you looked, I jumped onto Craigslist to see if anything was possible for me. Where could I go from there? As I searched around, I found job posts for administrative assistants and executive assistants drawing $45k, $65k, and even $85k. They were doing tasks that I was already good at. Hell, I had been a T.A. in high school and college, and I had picked up an administrative assistant/ receptionist role over the summers. Sure—I could do calendaring! I had been a financial advisor so, yeah, I could do expenses. In fact, I realized I could do everything they listed in the job descriptions. And I'd give *anything* to get a paycheck in my bank account every two weeks! As a fallback plan or maybe a steppingstone, it seemed like a good direction to go in.

So, I polished up my resume and went on countless interviews. I probably visited every recruiting and staffing agency around at the time. Some of them were brutal. Turned out my Chico past would haunt me. A typical conversation sounded something like:

"Your college GPA was 3.3? Well, okay. But—oh—you went to Chico? Forget it. My clients won't even touch you. They want Ivy League or 3.8+. Sorry. You'll have to look elsewhere."

And:

"Have you ever created a resume before?? It sure doesn't look like it. This is not impressing me."

That particular recruiter—I learned soon after—had a reputation within our community for being rude—so I wasn't the only one to suffer her disrespect. But the rest of them were equally as dismissive. The experience was utterly humiliating. My "screw you" attitude never seemed more appropriate and valid.

In spite of everything, I was able to find some temp and contract positions as an EA. I even held on to a couple of full-time positions for a while, but I would either quit or get fired. In the beginning, I was happy to have something I could just show up for, clock in, do the bare minimum, and then clock out and go home. It was straightforward, doable, and somewhat boring. It allowed me to maintain a comfortable, numbed-out cycle of working, going out to clubs, drinking, and getting high. Weekends were the only things I looked forward to; nothing else much mattered. I was escaping the bite of unresolved pain from many years past and continued to unabashedly and consistently indulge in self-sabotaging behaviors. I never realized that the common denominator in the whole mess was *me*.

Acknowledge the little steps along the way. In doing so, you will move from shame to self-worth, from secrecy to honesty, loneliness to connection with self and others, and from silence to having a voice.
—Janet Woititz

Would my path have been different if I hadn't been drinking and partying? Highly likely. But then I wouldn't be where I am today and have the opportunity to share my journey with you. The framework was there for me to succeed, but I was as yet unwilling to show up in a way that would result in success, for myself and others.

For the next four to five years, I partied. I went through the motions. I felt isolated and alone, self-sufficient but helpless. I couldn't see the point in anything. I shut down. I didn't know what it meant to relate to or connect with other people. I didn't ask people about themselves, their history, their family because I didn't want people asking me anything about me. Even today, when people say, "Where did you grow up? Where's your family?" a small part of me twinges for fear of being found out.

I was also bored as hell. There was one moment I'll never forget. I was sitting at my desk with the two phrases I emailed to people over and over and over again staring me in the face. I'd send them fifty times a day, literally.

Hi. Great to meet you via email. Would your calendar accommodate the following dates and times in here for a call with So & So?

Please let me know where there's alignment and I'll send an invite to confirm.

I felt like death warmed over. I felt like my brain was going to atrophy as I sat there, and all I could do was let it melt into a pile of grey sludge. It just seemed like such a huge waste of brain power. Now, don't get me wrong: it's gotta be done. It's all part of the job—and it's still part of my job today. (And, thankfully, these days, the task can be automated with a couple of clicks!) But, at the same time, if that was all that was going to be asked of me day after day, month after month, year after year, I couldn't survive it. I'm done. No, thank you.

I hated my role. I hated my job. What was the point? I felt stuck and trapped. I was sure I was a failure. I was done.

Burning Woman

After about five years of this slow, downward spiral of self-destruction, I hit rock bottom. There was nowhere further down than where I was. Emotionally and spiritually bankrupt, I gave zero fucks about anyone or anything—including me. My world felt like it was engulfed in flames and, due to my own blatant recklessness, I was going up in flames, too. It was a living hell, and I had no idea where the exit was. After all, I was just a victim of my circumstances, right?

But transformation can occur in spite of ourselves.

In the summer of 2013, I took myself to Burning Man, an annual nine-day art and musical festival of more than 70,000 people in the Nevada desert. I had gone for the last three years, and this time I was looking forward to seeing some old friends and having a lot of fun once again. A few days into the event, I bundled up in all sorts of furs and glittery garb, gathered with some people at the Esplanade, and took a hit of acid, hoping for a good ride.

The trip propelled me into a moment of intense clarity. In between rounds of laughing and crying, I had visions of some of my friends and acquaintances—all about the same age as me—getting married and buying houses, having kids, and building families. They had lives. They were stable. They seemed fairly happy.

Maggie, I thought, *You're just a loser sitting here, breathing in all this playa dust. You're just getting high and drinking every weekend. Now you're dropping acid. What the hell are you really doing with your life??*

And then I had a profound moment of clarity that I'll never forget. I realized how exhausted I was. I was spent from escaping; I was drained from numbing myself. I had nothing left. I was empty.

Something had to change. There *had* to be something more to my life than the endless spinning wheel of unconsciousness and meaninglessness. There *had* to be something bigger, something greater, something with a higher purpose available to me in my life.

It struck me that instant that I was done living life as I'd been living it. Life would never be the same for me.

It took a few more months for me to pull out of the cycle I had been locked into, but a few months later, I made the clear and present decision to get clean and sober. I was done with life as I knew it.

Now, this is not to suggest that everyone should go dropping acid for a moment of clarity. But if your life isn't where you want it to be, consider looking in the mirror. What's the common denominator? Are you drinking too much? Spending too much to fill a void? If something in your life isn't working, dig deep and stop looking for external forces to blame.

Ignition

I was in-between jobs at the time, so I started interviewing as much as I could, looking to find the right fit that didn't deaden me, didn't crush me. Something that would feel good and would even allow me to grow.

The dates escape me now, but at some point during my darkest days, I had been lucky enough to have a few chance exchanges on LinkedIn with Bonnie Low-Kramen, an international speaker and former personal assistant to Oscar-winning actress Olympia Dukakis. It was a connection that would significantly alter the trajectory of my life. I was still drinking and partying on weekends then, but I was winding down the behavior, and I knew it had to stop soon.

For some reason, Bonnie and I had a great connection on LinkedIn, so after a few exchanges back and forth, she asked me to meet her in New York City. Packing for the trip, I tried on countless shirt and pant combinations, trying to ignore my mind's cynical certainty that I was not good enough and that I was unworthy of anything she could offer me. *Why does she want to meet with me?* I wondered. *I don't have anything to wear. This is going to be awful!* I was lost in uncertainty.

When we met in New York in the lobby of a hotel, Bonnie was warm, kind, unassuming, curious—even loving. I remember experiencing something I rarely experience—feeling seen, heard, and understood in her presence. Of course, I was terribly nervous. I can't tell you exactly what we talked about or how it ended, but I must have made some sort of impression. As we talked, I sensed that

Bonnie picked up on my hunger for more, and she invited me to attend her two-day "Be the Ultimate Assistant" (BTUA) workshop in San Francisco, which I immediately signed up for.

BTUA was my first EA conference. This incredible course included a technology segment led by Vickie Sokol Evans, who is a masterful Microsoft-certified trainer as well as a trainer to Bill Gates' support team—so you know she's sharp. When I first saw Vickie's name on the speaking agenda, I thought to myself, *I'm leaving. Why would I stay for this? What do I need to learn about Microsoft? I don't need this.* But it turns out, I could not have been more wrong. I took back to the office a whole slew of skills that she taught. Later, I signed up for her RedCape Academy and every webinar she offered, and I immersed myself in every single training I could get my hands on that she delivered.

Together, Bonnie and Vickie created an alchemy of change in me. They ignited something in me that I didn't even know existed. Bonnie seemed to see something in me that I couldn't yet see in myself, and Vickie equipped me with the skills to elevate my work and the output of my organization. She also unleashed an as-yet-unknown insatiable curiosity that continues to propel me forward and blow the lid off of limitations I may have held for myself.

I have to admit, I gravitated towards Vickie. After all, you have to remember that I had few social skills or very little emotional intelligence at the time. I came off robotic and cold, and I made zero effort to connect with anyone. I thought that the keys to the kingdom were all about productivity and tools alone. So I gravitated towards Vickie, the keeper and teacher of the tools. Bonnie, on the other hand, was very much a people person and made everyone feel like they were the only person in the room when she was interacting 1:1 with someone.

The workshop got me excited about exploring and potentially mastering tools that are already at the fingertips of EAs like me, but we ignore or underutilize them. Tools that 99.9% of us aren't formally trained on how to use. We spend countless hours formatting documents unnecessarily—whether it's 20 minutes on a PowerPoint slide or two hours on a Word doc that can be formatted in less than five minutes.

From that introduction to the power of tools, I got passionate enough about Microsoft Office to later get certified in, which then allowed me to teach it to others.

With the gifts provided by these two women, you could say that seeds were planted in me, and over the next few years, I kept circling back. Even before attending BTUA, Bonnie was kind enough to introduce me to Jean Francese, who she described as "one of the best EAs in the country." Jean would also make it possible for me to land a new job that paid 40% more than my previous one.

I ate up every morsel of information I could at that workshop. I took notes, re-read my notes, and implemented as much as I could. They gave us a formula, and, by God, I was going to follow it. I was incredibly hungry for an avenue out of my world. I knew there was more out there for me, I just didn't know what it was or how I was going to get there.

Don't let your past determine your present and future.

Just Two Minutes

And I wasn't going to get there in a straight line. During the first day of the workshop, Bonnie invited all of us to get on the following day's schedule to give a two-minute presentation and demonstrate and share our favorite hack, app, or productivity tool with our fellow EAs.

Two minutes. That's doable, right?

So that night, I devoted some time preparing handouts about the importance of customizing LinkedIn invitations when requesting to connect with folks. I wanted people to be able to take them home and apply my suggestions once they returned home. I knew my material; I was living and breathing the topic every day. So, needless to say, I was confident and ready to deliver.

Or so I thought. When it was my turn to present, I walked up to the stage and found myself in front of a room full of high-level executives and personal assistants. There I was, handouts in hand, ready to talk about a topic I knew intimately. But just thirty seconds into what was supposed to be a two-minute demo, time stood still. That notorious frog arrived in my throat. Like an out-of-body experience, I watched as my chest tightened, my voice quivered, and my hands trembled violently. Unable to get another word out, I took my seat and hung my head in utter humiliation and defeat.

I figured my fate was sealed. But at the close of the workshop, somebody actually came up to me and told me not to let this one failure stop me. "You know your material, but something's getting stuck *right here*," she said, pointing to my throat. I'll never forget it. When I asked her what I could do about it, all she said was that she thought a therapist could help me.

This kind person had pointed out something that was true about me: my voice was stuck. My ability to express myself in the world was trapped. And when I looked back at my life, I realized I had never been taught to speak up or express myself. I didn't have a safe environment to be vulnerable. I had never been taught to establish healthy boundaries or taught how to say "No."

Now, I'm not saying that all EAs are exactly like me and are not strong in expressing themselves, but I do think that many of us—because we're in a role to serve another—often think we're essentially the "help." We think that our opinions don't matter. But that couldn't be further from the truth.

Plus, one of the reasons I became an EA was to limit my visibility and to *avoid* having to do anything so vulnerable as public speaking and presenting. My current job worked for me precisely because I didn't have to talk to people or be vulnerable in front of people. I could hide behind a screen, and no one would ask too much of me. But, then, there I was, talking to people and being vulnerable.

That night, I decided I was never going to let myself go through that kind of humiliation and failure again. I realized I needed to commit myself to a new course of action and actively pursue training in public speaking. So, ironically enough, my crushing failure actually got me to strap myself into the driver's seat of my own life as comfortably as I could and deciding the direction I actually wanted to go in—for the very first time in my life. Ready or not, I was setting myself on a new course for the ride of my life.

3
RELENTLESS PURSUIT

After crashing and burning at BTUA, I started looking for ways to bolster my ability to speak in public. At first, my single-minded goal was to simply make it through my next public speaking opportunity without being forced to sit down from debilitating anxiety. I found Magnetic Speaking, a public speaking training company in San Francisco, founded by Peter Khoury. Once I took that course, I would never look back. In BTUA, Bonnie and Vickie had awakened within me an insatiable hunger to learn, to grow, and to see how far I could stretch. Magnetic Speaking helped me become a person who could make a difference in the world.

Magnetic Speaking

The Magnetic Speaking weekend bootcamps and one-hour mini-workshops in the mornings were tough on me. Sitting alongside the other participants in the class, I felt like a fraud. Hello imposter syndrome all over again. The classes were largely comprised of entrepreneurs and founders of tech startups—people who regularly delivered presentations and met with investors, people who were looking to hone their crafts. Many shared with the rest of us about the projects they were working on. Of course, I didn't have anything to speak about. I figured nobody wanted to hear about calendaring, travel, and expenses. As an executive assistant, I was out of my element. *Who the hell wants to hear about my role as an EA?* I thought.

Feeling like a longshot, I'd go to the bootcamps when I felt like it or when schedules permitted. Then I'd take some time off. There was no consistency in my life at the time; I was flying by the seat of my pants.

But the training eventually kicked in and reshaped how I am in the world. It didn't flip a switch—unfortunately, I wasn't turned into a successful public speaker overnight. The experience was nerve-wracking, confronting, frustrating, and challenging. But the moment that I heard Peter tell the class that public speaking is the new "glass ceiling," it hit a nerve in me. I wasn't going to let somebody else's limitations stop me—my own were hard enough to deal with.

The program was so transformative for me that, over the next five years, I would spend more than 50 hours in the Magnetic Speaking bootcamp programs, gaining confidence, and honing my skills so I could speak my truth, share my skills, experience and learnings. Then, when I got my Microsoft Office Specialist certification a couple years later, I started to discover that I could be a "natural" at it. With a certain expertise within my grasp, I found I could speak about it. Teach about it. Effectively. Competently. Confidently. And that's when things really started to take off. But more about that later.

Not About Me

After the BTUA conference, Bonnie and Jean knew I was on the fence about attending the next learning opportunity for me. The conference would be an event designed for senior executive assistants and celebrity assistants, and it was just what I needed next. They encouraged me to attend and said it would change my life. Costing $3000 all-in to fly across the country for a two-day executive assistant program—without reimbursement—it would be my first major investment in myself outside of college.

The people on the agenda at the conference were forces in and of themselves: Ann Hyatt, then chief of staff to Eric Schmidt of Google; Anikka Fragodt, Mark Zuckerberg's former EA for many years; and Robin Guido, EA to Parker Harris, co-founder of Salesforce.

Talk about a lineup of power players. In my usual self-defeated way, I figured I was *way* out of my league.

But at every event I attend, I walk away with at least one golden nugget that later becomes the defining moment of the trip. This time it was Robin Guido's presentation that opened the doors in my mind to what was possible.

Robin told us about her first annual vision statement that she ever submitted to her employer at Salesforce. The company uses a system they call "V2MOM" for "vision, values, methods, obstacles and measures," and they ask their employees to fill in what those are for them. Her initial V2MOM looked more like a job description than a vision statement. She was all about the tasks: "book the most efficient flights under budget," and "find the least expensive hotel." But when Parker, her exec, read it, he offered her a higher vision of her job. His words became a mantra for me:

"No. That's not it," he said after reading her V2MOM. "Your role is to help me reach my next level."

My role is to help my executive reach their next level, I said to myself, letting it sink in.

That short statement was absolutely the single most powerful thing I heard that weekend. It gave me a new understanding of my job—one that opens doors instead of shuts them. It helped me see my EA role as doing what I can to help my executive reach their next level. And here I had been thinking, *Is this all there is to this job?* The answer was: No—there's a *lot* more available to you.

I started to consider that the role of an EA has little do with me and everything to do with them. That perspective moves me out of a space of entitlement and into one where I'm figuring out how I can add value and deliver at a higher level. Making them more effective and efficient in their role also means that I'm more successful, too. Up until that point, I had never really understood the magnitude of what my role could encompass, if I chose it.

This job has little to do with me and everything to do with lifting my executive to their next level.

I got it and I committed to it. I had been living in a world of the EA *ordinary*—travel, expenses, calendaring; travel, expenses, calendaring—and I felt like a whole new world of *extraordinary* had just opened up for me.

I wanted to thank Robin, but again, the lines to speak with her were long, and I tend to be fairly impatient, to say the least. Admittedly, if I had reached the front of the line, I didn't know what I would have said, didn't think it was important enough, and felt like I would have wasted her time. So, I didn't meet her that day. But I never forgot the impact Robin's words had on my trajectory. I figured that one day I'd have the opportunity to thank her and share what I heard—but I couldn't have imagined in a million years what would transpire several years after first hearing her speak.

When I returned home from that conference, I realized that something had shifted in me and the way I work. My thinking evolved from:

"What's in it for me?" "What do I get out of this?" "What's the point?"

to:

"How will this affect my executive and my organization?" "How can I serve the greater good?" "What can I do?" "Where can I improve and make enhancements?" "What more can I do?"

Think about it. Which person would you rather work with? The one thinking, "What's in it for me?" or the one asking themselves, "Where can I do more?" If you were an exec, which one would you rather have serving as an extension of you? Which one would you want to compensate highly, send to training, and continually invest in—feeling confident that they're going to deliver to you, the organization, and its stakeholders?

I realized that I could fulfill my role as an EA in a more satisfying and elevated way than I ever had—by serving others and ensuring they have what they need when they need it. By helping them deliver on their own commitments to internal and external stakeholders. My job can be to elevate their reach, their presence, their voice, and their brand in whatever capacity or context is called for. I can do it by taking care of whatever needs to be done, which allows them to focus on realizing the vision for the organization.

It was one more breakthrough for me, and I had to express my thanks. Two years later, I would send Robin a Thank You note and share with her the impact her talk at the conference had on my career. By the way, I didn't ask her to meet for coffee or to pick her brain. I didn't ask her to help me out. I reached out and emailed her a note just to say "Thanks." I had no expectations.

> We've not yet met, but your presentation at BEL in NJ was one I'll never forget. Your talk—and slide, in particular—about your KPO/KPIs working with Parker was an "ah-ha" moment for me. Being in this role has little to do with me and everything to do with helping our executives reach their next level. The mental shift I experienced that day has had a tremendous impact on my career trajectory and where I am today.
>
> Thank you, Robin.
> —Maggie Jacobs

And then she replied back.

She told me it was one of kindest notes she'd ever gotten. Then she told me that she had a speaking gig in a few months and asked me if I'd mind taking a look at some of her slides. She wanted me to give *her* some feedback. *Robin Guido* was asking *me* for help. So, of course I said "Yes" and agreed to meet with her for coffee and give her my two cents.

Somewhere in that conversation, I also apparently shared with Robin that I eventually wanted a role that was more challenging for me than the one I had, one where I could step into my strengths and play a little bigger. While I don't even remember that share now, it was because of it that Robin would call me up a year or two later and tap me for a role that I would have never even considered possible for me. Just wait.

Libby

Then I met Libby Moore.

The following year, I attended an EA seminar where I first heard and finally met Libby Moore. Libby spoke on the panel the first day of the event and did a keynote on the second day. When I heard her speak, I thought, *Wow, she's authentic and real. I can feel her humanness. I'd love to meet her.* But, alas, there was a long line of people waiting to meet her after the event, and it was more than I was willing to wait through. *Besides*, I thought, *What would I even say when I got to the front of the line?* I had no idea.

Libby's a certified life coach and Oprah's former chief of staff of 11 years. That first evening, I had a diabolical case of imposter syndrome running in full force in my head. *What the hell am I doing at an EA conference with 250 C-suite EAs?* I asked myself. *I don't belong here! Surely, they'll figure out who I am, where I came from, and what I've done—and ban me for life!* That was the war in my head. Day in and day out.

The next morning, still crippled with self-doubt, I stared at myself in the mirror, my head recounted more debilitating thoughts. *You're not supposed to be here! Pack your bags and go home! They're on to you. Who do you think you are coming here? You're not adding any value. Leave. Now.*

How vicious we can be to ourselves! Could you imagine socializing with someone who speaks to you this way day in and day out? Or spending every waking moment with them? Absolutely not. Then why would you allow yourself to let your internal dialogue influence how you show up in the world?

Then, Amy Cuddy's Ted Talk came to my mind. In the last seven minutes of Amy's talk, she tells her own personal story about being dogged by thoughts of, "I'm not supposed to be here." And I saw her in me. So, I followed her guidance. I pointed at myself in the mirror and firmly said, "I *am* supposed to be here. I belong here! I am a C-suite EA, and I'm going to go downstairs and be a part of this!" Who has time for those self-defeating thoughts? Not me!

It starts with you. We become what we think about.
Change your thoughts, change your life.

By the time I made my way to the hall where breakfast was served, everyone else was seated in the ballroom—everyone but one person who was also looking for a seat. Who was that? Libby Moore.

Like magic, what I had asked the universe for just the previous day—to meet Libby—was now happening in living color before me. Then, the self-sabotaging mental dialogue started up again. *What would she want with me? Who am I, anyway? Nobody!* We made eye contact, exchanged morning pleasantries, and made our way with our plates into the ballroom where everybody else was already seated and eating their breakfast. As we made our way in, it became clear that there was only one table with more than one unoccupied seat left, so we both headed there. We sat down.

I was finally starting to wake up and get excited for the day. I was sharing breakfast with Libby Moore and five or so other EAs! Life was good!

When it was time to enter the conference room, being a creature of habit, I wound my way around to the same table I had sat the day before. And who do I find there? Libby Moore again! It was the third time in less than an hour that I "bumped into" her. The universe was clearly lining something up. My curiosity got the best of me. I thought, *Ok! I'll play ball!* My intuition was hinting that there was something here—some connection—to be explored, but I had no idea what it might be. Then, at some point in the day, Bonnie Kramen delivered her session and asked everyone in the room a question.

"How many of you have mentors?"

Less than half of the hands in the room went up. Libby didn't raise her hand, either. I knew enough about Libby to know that she was venturing into a new chapter of her professional coaching and speaking work. I wondered, *How could she do this without a mentor? She must have a master plan. I'm going to ask.*

The audacity. I shock myself at times. I slid her a note across the table.

Now I don't know about you, but my penmanship is crap. Chalk it up to learning to type at a young age. Needless to say, I was nervous as hell, asking—with nearly illegible handwriting—Oprah's former Chief of Staff how she's building her brand! A pile of crumpled pieces of paper was collecting next to me from writing and rewriting the note to Libby. Thankfully, her back was toward me, so she couldn't see the mess I was making on the table.

I worked up the courage to finally slide my good-enough note across the table to her, tapping her on the shoulder. She looked at me inquisitively. She glanced at the note, looked up at me, tilted her head, looked down at the note, and paused. I swear time stood still. She finally looked up, pointed at me, and broadly mouthed the words, "YOU are!"

Whoa. *Not* what I expected. Then again, I don't know what I was expecting. Some part of me simply knew that Libby needed to be on LinkedIn, and now, due to acting on something I can only describe as what I was pulled to do, I was going to participate in the process.

So, I helped Libby build her LinkedIn profile. Since then, she continues to remind me that she's on the platform "because of YOU, Maggie!" Since she had worked for Oprah, building out her social networks hadn't been a priority. But with some persistence and assistance, she's now on LinkedIn and thriving. Through that single act of boldness, I'm grateful to say something incredible emerged. Since then, Libby has become a friend, mentor, coach, and trusted advisor. Through her kind and patient guidance, I've had incredible conversations and realizations that I may not have had otherwise. Among other things, she was instrumental in instilling in me the confidence to ask for my first salary increase.

Be bold. Follow the voice the pulls you, not the one that hinders you. There are times when a force truly greater than yourself compels you to act. Be open. Allow it. Do it. Watch the magic unfold.

Salesforce

I never thought a company like Salesforce would ever ask me to interview for a job. One of those big shiny companies? Are you kidding? They had approached me in 2015, and when I drove over for the interview, I first sat in my car in the basement of the parking lot of the corporate office, trembling because it was such an enormous company. But once I got inside and sat down with the exec, I realized I didn't get the "vibe" that seemed to always tell me that I'm going to work well with somebody. It just wasn't there. We didn't resonate. Oh well.

When I got home that day, I told my husband, Scott, that the interview had fallen flat, and I didn't think I wanted to bother to continue with the interview process. But Scott disagreed.

"I think you should just go and find out. Who's to know where it would lead?" he asked me presciently.

I got called back to interview at Salesforce several more times and made it all the way up to become their second choice for the job. All in all, I felt that I hit it off quite well with just about everyone I had spoken with—with the exception of the one person that I would support in the job. But that series of interviews would end up opening the door for my opportunity to work for a growing tech company that would have just the right fit for me.

6sense

I didn't even actually apply for the job. In fact, I didn't need a job at all. But the irony is that when you don't need a job, that's when you kick ass in the interview. You're not desperate, you're relaxed and more authentic, and it works because you're not just selling them trying to get out of your current situation, they have to sell to you, too.

Even though I was pretty happy in my job, I would continue passively take calls as LinkedIn inquiries came in. One day, I happened to find an article that told the story of Amanda Kahlow, CEO of a tech firm, and how she won over the CMO of Salesforce with an ad hoc pitch she made in the women's locker room of a swanky high-end club in San Francisco. I found Amanda's profile online and liked her immediately. She seemed to be a force for good, a female founder, helping women in her community. She practiced yoga, she meditated—she just sounded amazing, and I was intrigued. Her story fired me up, so I dug deeper online. There I discovered a posting for an EA to the CEO and the SVP of Sales at her company, 6sense.

I took some time to peruse her profile on LinkedIn, as well as that of the SVP of Sales. Not long after that, I got a message from Pablo Pollard, the SVP of Sales at 6sense. Noticing that I had viewed his profile, he had looked me up. His message was simple:

"Hey, Maggie. We're looking for an incredible EA. Could this be you?"

We scheduled a call and talked for a while. After a short discussion, he got to the point.

"So... what do you think?" he asked me.

"Pablo, I gotta be honest with you! This job sounds exactly like me. It's got my name all over it." And that was true.

He sounded pleased. "Well, I'd love to bring you in to meet you in person—but there's just one snag. A few of us will be leaving for Burning Man in a few days."

I smiled to myself. My skin tingled with an intuitive knowing that I was going to end up working for this company. After all, I knew Burning Man, and I knew how unusual yet how perfect it was that these people were going to it, too. Once again, the stars were aligning. I could feel it.

So we waited until they were back in town, and I met with Pablo and Amanda the following Tuesday morning at 7 a.m. The interview experience was nothing short of surreal for me. Never have I had a more positive and engaging interview experience where I could actually feel the connection, alignment, and excitement for what the future holds. The three of us talked openly and authentically about everything that mattered. We resonated with each other. After only about 45 minutes, Amanda put the question on the table:

"Well, Maggie," she said. "I can tell Pablo likes you. I like you. What do *you* think?"

And there it was. You know those stories you occasionally hear about people getting offers on the spot? I never believed that it actually happens in real life. Well it does. At 7:45 a.m. on that very Tuesday morning, we hugged each other goodbye, and I left, got in my car and just burst into tears. I was on cloud nine.

I received their offer a couple hours later.

But here's what really caught my attention. The reason why it all went so swimmingly didn't become clear until a couple days later when I talked to Pablo. Turns out, Salesforce had been an investor in 6sense; and the company's sales team was made up entirely of Salesforce alum. I mentioned to Pablo that I had interviewed there a few months back, and his response knocked me on my heels.

"Oh, I know!" he said. "I talked to every single mutual connection that we have, Maggie. And every single one of them said that you're wonderful, you're hungry, and you're driven. They all said they just didn't think that you'd be a culture fit with them. And I thought, 'That's perfect. I don't want someone who fits the Salesforce culture. I want to hire her for 6sense.'"

The lesson? Put yourself out there. Clearly, if I hadn't gone through all those interviews at Salesforce, who knows if things would have fallen into place as well as they did with 6sense!

RedCape

In 2016, I took the next step to build my EA skills and signed up for Vickie Sokol Evans' RedCape Academy, a one-year ninja skill-building in Microsoft—to learn everything that none of us were taught in school. The program upgraded my Microsoft technical chops and equipped me with the skills to later deliver team trainings to the tune of six-figure savings of time and money. I now consider it one of my best investments in terms of the value I bring to any organization I work for. I used to just plan QBRs and SKOs. Today, I speak at them, delivering Microsoft tools training and enablement sessions. I still receive texts today thanking me for trainings I delivered years ago on what I learned from Vickie's courses. Forget the hours already wasted pouring over formatting slides, docs, and tables. You can really save hundreds of hours over your lifetime. The courses propel you forward like nothing else.

Robin Calls

And sometimes other people see something in you that you can't yet see in yourself. Near the end of 2017, Robin Guido reached out to me. Now, when Robin Guido, executive administrator to the co-founder of Salesforce, knocks on my door—I answer.

Robin said she had something to run by me, and she wanted to talk. I wasn't looking to leave my current post at the time and working for a massive company like Salesforce didn't interest me in the slightest. Minutes before I got on the call, full of resistance, I said to my husband, "I don't want to work at Salesforce, Scott! I've been through this already! It's not going to happen. It's a waste of time."

In his wisdom, Scott said, "Maggie, it's just a call. Aren't you the one who encourages others to 'take the call'? Take your own advice."

"Fine. The only way I'd even *remotely* consider anything at Salesforce would be if it's in Product," I told him.

So, I took the call. After we exchanged pleasantries, Robin explained the reason she was reaching out.

"Maggie, a couple of years ago, I remember you telling me you wanted to do more, do something that challenges you, something where you could really step into your skill set."

Remember that conversation I had with her over coffee two years before, when I mentioned I wanted more of a challenge? Well, Robin did.

"You were the first external person that came to my mind when something opened up here at Salesforce," she continued. "It's a big job, and I think you have the chutzpah to be successful in this role."

"Robin, I'm flattered. Truly," I told her sincerely. "But I'm happy where I am, and I don't want to work at a company of 17,000 people."

"Well, we're actually at 30,000 today, Maggie. But let me tell you about the role."

The role was to support Brett Taylor. Do you know who Brett Taylor is? He is co-founder of Google Maps, former CTO at Facebook, and founder and CEO of Quip, which Salesforce had recently bought for $750M. He's also the Chief *Product* Officer of Salesforce. (*Remember how I said I'd only consider a job in Product?*)

"Robin, would this person get to work with you?" I asked.

"Well Maggie, as of matter of fact, this person would sit next to me."

When I got off the phone, I was crying. *Are you kidding me? Support a Chief at one monster of a company like Salesforce? How could this be happening?* It sure didn't feel real. I could hear my husband laughing at me from the other room.

"Dude, do you get it yet? Or do you still not see it?"

I looked up the job req online. "Senior Executive Assistant to the Chief Product Officer." Now, I never would have applied to the position myself much less had the confidence to think I'd make it past an initial screening. But there I was. Being tapped by the most influential EA in the massive company.

Still feeling ambivalent about the job, I agreed to take the interview. I wasn't going to become the person I wanted to become by sitting in my current role doing nothing. My goal for the experience was to soak up as much information as I could from this legendary figure within our community. I certainly wasn't expecting anything more than that.

Salesforce didn't make me an offer then, and, honestly, I was relieved. Perhaps my ambivalence was palpable and off-putting. I was anything but fired up—an attitude that's not so attractive to a hiring manager. But an offer would have caused me to make one of the most difficult decisions I'd ever had to make. I was on the fence.

Invite failure. Learn and grow from it. Allow it to fuel your fire.

4
I'M NOT LEAVING

So I landed an incredible job with an exciting, cutting-edge tech company, and I was feeling more fulfilled than I ever thought possible. We were involved in projects that benefited the community and supported women's and girl's empowerment, and I loved that. Our CEO was on the speaker circuit, speaking at events like Further Future, events that featured speakers such as Alphabet's Chairman and former Google CEO, Eric Schmidt. It was incredible!

But some things were starting to feel uncomfortable for me. I looked around and noticed that the tasks that I was doing and the errands I was running were seriously underutilizing me with respect to my skillset, hunger, and drive. Only certain people were allowed to ask me for anything; the rest were told to fend for themselves. While I was making some impactful contributions of my own choosing, I found myself more like an errand girl in my day to day—fetch breakfast, lunch, snacks, dry cleaning, walk the dog. I was feeling exhausted, getting spread too thin, and treading water in what felt like an ocean of chaos. I felt like I had been dropped into scenes of *The Devil Wears Prada.* Demeaned and humiliated too much of the time. It was my new reality.

News got around to me that my predecessor had quit after only six months on the job. She didn't even bother to give her two weeks' notice, apparently. Somebody told me it was because she wanted her self-respect back, and I was starting to see why. More and more, I was put in positions that were compromising my own integrity, my name, my brand. It was going beyond where I was willing to go.

At one point, a colleague put it all into perspective for me. "Maggie," he said, "it's a mind fuck." I realized it wasn't just me, after all.

Then there was a shake-up at the top, and an executive reorg became a reality. It was spring, and the new CEO, along with three members of his "proven" team, were slated to join us. That meant we'd get four new chiefs to onboard—and I was not excited about it. I really wasn't up for the catastrophe I could see coming, and I definitely wanted no part of the incoming CEO. I wasn't going to stick around for the party. I was outta there.

Earlier in the year, Dasha Vasilyeva, a friend and colleague who had, several years before, worked with 6sense's incoming CEO had asked me if I might stick around to work with him. I curtly replied, "Nope." She insisted he was great and asked me to simply be open to the idea. "Maggie, these are *real* executives, they're world-class leaders." But I was not open, nor did I intend to be. The thought of navigating the politics and being caught in the middle of a transition, reorg, and the inevitable cross-fire made my skin crawl. I was convinced it'd be political suicide. I was more than ready to move on to my next chapter. The new guy was taking his sweet time doing his due diligence—so, I figured, I could go interview and do my *own* kind of due diligence elsewhere.

It was only a matter of finding my next executive.

Last Days

There I was: the 18-month chapter of my life working for 6sense looked like it was coming to a close. The new CEO announced his impending arrival, and it was one of my last days on the job. I had been offered an opportunity to work at a company that was closer to home, had a CEO who seemed to have a firm grasp of what "partnership" meant, and with whom I had great chemistry. And I was taking it.

But the new guy, Jason Zintak, formerly chief sales officer at Responsys and former CEO at Platfora, kept coming around. He was kind, warm, authentic, transparent—even had a certain gravitas. You know how you can sometimes read someone in 30 seconds? He passed my initial intuitive test—and then he kept passing it. Unlike my experience with some of the people I interviewed with and previous executives I've worked with, I never felt like I was just "the help" around Jason. He communicated. He was clear. He was looking for ways to make things operate on higher levels. He asked great questions, *and* he listened. After three to five interactions with Jason, I started thinking that maybe I didn't have to be completely closed to the idea of sticking around after all.

He came in for our All Hands meeting on a Friday for the formal announcement. He held the floor for 30 minutes, spoke about his background, why he joined, and his vision for our future. He was engaging, transparent, articulate—and, I had to admit, likable.

The walls that protect you also imprison you.

A few colleagues knew I was leaving, and one of them reached out to him directly, encouraging him to save me. I have to admit, my curiosity was piqued from his talk, so, as he was leaving, I decided to walk him out.

"Maggie, I understand you're leaving," he said. "I didn't pick up on that at all. Is there anything we can do to save you?"

"Sure. We can talk," I said. I figured I could at least give him the courtesy of a meeting. But we'd have to meet that weekend, since I would be starting my new role the following Wednesday.

Are We Doing This?

So, I met with Jason that Sunday. To that meeting, I brought with me two things: a deck and a book. When I interview, I almost always bring a book and sometimes a deck as a leave-behind, and this was no exception. I do it both to set myself apart and to help execs understand what the EA role is really all about and how critical it is to their success. When I met with the CPO at Salesforce, a company of 30,000 people at the time, I even brought a deck explaining how their EAs could use their own product to their advantage, and I tried to inform him about the impact it could have on the EAs there. I know, ballsy, right?

When we conquer our fears, we discover a boundless, bottomless, inexhaustible well of passion.

The deck I brought to Jason was about an EA's role navigating change management, and it described how Jason could lean on me—theoretically—as a motivator and a connector. After all, I knew everyone in the organization, and he hardly knew anyone yet. Plus, I pointed out that with change comes opportunity. With a reorg, everyone has a target on their back. It gives us an opportunity to step up and really show what we're capable of—or make an exit if we're dissatisfied—but the choice is ours to make.

The book I brought him was Jan Jones' *The CEO's Secret Weapon: How Great Leaders and Their Assistants Maximize Productivity and Effectiveness,* and I had it all highlighted and with tons of sticky tabs sticking out of its pages.

I also brought my most recent and best LinkedIn recommendations.

"Wow. You actually *think* like this?" he asked me, looking surprised, looking at the "gifts" I brought.

Jason asked me to tell him what happened at 6sense for me—what went wrong. "Was there something specific that happened?" Why was I so motivated to fly? He wanted to know.

I appreciated his interest in the details. "This isn't the role I interviewed for," I told him, "and it's not conducive to a healthy and productive work environment. Eighteen months? I'm good. It's time for me to move on."

Then he put the question on the table: "If you *were* to stay, Maggie, could you give me a month—two months tops—to put you in a better environment?"

"Sure." He was starting to win me over.

We talked. As I was painfully aware of the chaos that loomed in the organization, I wondered if he really had any idea what he was getting himself into. But I kept it positive.

"Tell me about your favorite EAs you've worked with," I suggested. My intention was to understand how he worked with them, find out how he perceived the partnership, and to get a sense of how we might work together, if we were in fact to work together. He told me he had always inherited EAs, but he starting to think that he hadn't ever really leveraged the potential of working with an EA before. He had no idea what he didn't know.

So, I pulled out all the stops. I shared with him the value I can bring and what I can do. And that's when I brought out the book.

"This articulates the art of the possible," I said.

We talked some more, and I was honest with him. If he really wanted me to stay, I'd need his help with three things: 1) keeping my integrity in light of having just signed on with another company, 2) beating or matching my current offer, and 3) promising to shift certain conditions in a way that gets me out of the fire completely. He agreed and promised.

"So… are… we… doing this?" he asked me.

Now, there are pivotal moments we all have in our lives that simply alter the course of everything that comes after. Had I not met Jason at that precise time, I wouldn't have found myself on a path that ultimately enriched me in so many ways. The trainings, the opportunities, the people, and the personal and professional growth have been nothing short of spectacular since that moment. And this was just the beginning.

Almost before he finished the question, grinning from ear to ear, I blurted out, "Yes!"

Reorg from Hell

But reorgs can be hell. Even if you're working with an exec you admire and respect, reorgs can go on and on and no one knows exactly what's happening or what to expect. It's like you're sitting on the tarmac in the middle of summer in a hot, hot, super humid city. The plane is delayed, the A/C is broken, and you're squirming in your seat, wanting things to happen a lot faster than they are. The pilot keeps saying that it's going to be only 10 more minutes, only 10 more minutes, only 10 more. But minutes, hours, days, even months go by. (The reorg, not the plane.)

Some of us had been promised certain things and we were waiting and waiting for those promises to be delivered. Many of us wanted to scream and yell and swear, but we just couldn't. They were incredibly frustrating times for just about everyone. And I was still experiencing the most challenging and chaotic professional working relationship I've had in my entire career with some people in the organization.

But the universe, in all its wisdom, had my path cross with that of Jorah Ryken, who I hired in May 2017 as a coach to help me work through the chaos of the reorg at the company. As an EA herself, she had weathered five CFOs over 15 years, so she knew exactly what I was going through. Jorah reminded me to breathe. From time to time, she talked me off the ledge. But most importantly, she told me that, as much as I might want to say something, my best play was to keep my mouth shut and keep my thoughts to myself. Had I not gotten that advice, I can't be sure that I'd still be employed at 6sense today. Having a coach and being able to vent and ask for guidance, sometimes multiple times per week, was essential for me to survive.

In the meantime, the volume of my work was spiraling out of control. I found myself always on—answering emails, texts, and Slacks from 7 a.m. to 10 p.m., and sometimes later. Since we were a small shop, we didn't have an HR, IT, or Facilities to help things run smoothly. Any time anyone needed something, whether exec- or office-related, they'd come to me or our office assistant. But mostly to me. I was more familiar. I was the comfortable choice. Combine that with three execs in high demand and you get a recipe for failure. I constantly felt like I was dropping the ball and wasn't able to respond to people well enough. And if I didn't respond to emails right away, people would stop by my desk. Which of course ate up precious time.

Now, in my mind, I've always wanted to support just one person, the CEO, because the more people you support, the more the quality and effectiveness of your work diminishes. But now, due to the tsunami of shifting tides, I was supporting three executives—yet still doing my best to support the new CEO's success in every way possible. While I've always considered our role as EAs was to fix things, minimize chaos, and anticipate issues before they arise, it became literally impossible to do. I was getting tremendous pressure coming from everywhere. I kept track of some of the traffic and noted I was averaging about 75 asks per day, often times many more. It was absolute insanity.

Still, I kept my mouth shut. I suffered in silence. I was the strong, silent type, I guess, and it just invited more pressure and more exhaustion. Internally, I became a hateful, miserable bitch. Looking back, I think the lesson is to always communicate. Turns out that when we do finally get the courage to speak up, it's at least three months beyond when we should have actually asked. Too many of us wait too long to get help from others. I sure did. But more about that later.

Asserting Myself

When Jason started, I had his agreement that I would get to play at a higher level, and I began inserting myself into every leadership meeting that he went to. I didn't wait for him to ask me, and I didn't ask if I could attend. I just showed up. After all, I'm the EA to the CEO; I'm his right hand, and my thinking was—*This is how it's going down*. I was able to architect my role right from the start, doing what I thought would empower me to serve him and our team best. There was one meeting that he predicted would be a snooze fest for me because I didn't have the technical chops to follow the discussion. And he rightly said that I didn't need to be in that meeting if I didn't want to. I thanked him graciously and chose not to attend. But then something changed. For the next six months, I didn't get invited back to any of the executive meetings—and it started to mess with my head. I started to think, *Oh my God. He doesn't like me! He doesn't want to work with me! I'm going to get fired!* I started to catastrophize the whole thing.

Annoyed after months of feeling sidelined, I sent Jason an article by another Hallie Warner's exec, Adam Hergenrother, titled "Why CEOs Need a Chief of Staff and an Executive Assistant," which I thought did a good job of (re)articulating the value that EAs bring. It asserted that EAs should be in all the leadership meetings as a presence to capture action items and owners and to follow up with deliverables and deadlines. I sent it to him at 6:15 in the morning stating, "For our 1:1 today and future discussions re executing your vision." Fifteen minutes later, I got a response from him.

"Cool!!" he said.

What a turd, I thought. *He didn't even read it. Why is he patronizing me?*

A few hours later, I got another email from him. "Hey, can you attend tomorrow's leadership meeting?"

It blew my mind. I saw that *I* had put *myself* into a shitstorm of my own making, thinking that he didn't want me and that I wasn't welcome. I *was* welcome; I just shouldn't expect an invitation. I realized that executives aren't thinking about us, nor should they be. Our role is to elevate them—not the other way around. I could choose for myself and act independently. Lesson learned. From then on, I sat in on every executive meeting. My choice.

> *Just because you haven't been invited doesn't mean you're not welcome.*

Finding my Voice

2017 was the year I found my voice. Once I spoke up, things started to happen. Of course, they didn't happen overnight because things never happen overnight in companies, right? We're not talking Amazon Prime. But it was impactful. Once I started speaking up, it got easier. I started asking for resources and investment in my own trainings. I would say, "Hey, I need this and here's why...." I started standing up for myself, asking for what I wanted to ask for, being willing to risk hearing a "No." (Although, I have to admit that I've also trained myself – this context – to hear a "No" as meaning, "Not right now." So, in my mind, only rarely did I let doors of opportunity close completely.)

So, guess who was finally listening to me? *Me.*

Most importantly, my years of investing in myself were paying off. I had failed spectacularly, and yet I learned to take responsibility for my failures and find the lesson in them. At first, I was only willing to see a few redeeming qualities within myself, but I took what little I found, and I paid it forward towards my own future. When opportunity knocked, I answered, and by putting one foot in front of the other, I gathered skills, confidence, resources, and, finally, experience and expertise. A lot of it wasn't easy or fun, but today I can say that I'm a thriving example of what's possible when you take radical, intentional action. I look back now, and I wouldn't change a thing.

To not own your reality or to not speak your truth is the ultimate act of betrayal to yourself...
Acknowledge the little steps along the way.
In doing so, you will move from shame to self-worth, from secrecy to honesty, loneliness to connection with self and others, and from silence to having a voice.
–Julie D. Bowden

5
EVEN LEADERSHIP

So, how did I go from being a quiet assistant to leading trainings and speaking in front of hundreds of people? It may have taken five years, but I kept going back to Magnetic Speaking bootcamps, watching, listening, learning, and improving my public speaking skills, drinking in more than 50 hours' worth of intense trainings. For a long time, I felt like an outsider. While other participants had fascinating topics in tech, business, and operations to speak about, I didn't think I had much of anything to share. But in 2016, I got my Microsoft Office Specialist (MOS) certification, which gave me some expertise in Microsoft products and tools. That changed everything for me.

Finally, I had something I could talk about at Magnetic Speaking bootcamps. I started giving mini Microsoft Office trainings at my speaking opportunities in class. Turns out, the other participants were largely Google-lovers and Microsoft-haters so I got their attention by mapping out all the things you actually can do with Microsoft, like how to format a Word document or Excel spreadsheet in less than five minutes. As I talked, people's eyes got bigger and bigger, and I knew I was hitting home. Then they started asking me if I worked at Microsoft or if we could meet for coffee afterwards, wanting more. And I started to think I've actually got something here.

When it comes to public speaking, it's all about knowing your material. If you know what you're talking about, and you have a valuable message to deliver, there's little to no anxiety beforehand. You know you have something of value to share. And I did. So things finally started to get easier and easier for me. I could share, I could teach, I could make a difference and make an impact. Now, that was different!

> *Success on any major scale requires you to accept responsibility.*
> *—Michael Korda,*
> *Simon & Schuster*

My MOS training was a game-changer. 6sense is an Office 365 shop, and the training quickly turned me into the in-house Microsoft expert. I started to notice that the sales proposal templates my colleagues were using were a huge pain in the ass. People had to manually format words and shift lines over—the insanity was mind-boggling to me! And so I thought, *You know what, I'm going to take this form and I'm going to redesign it!* I used the developer feature in Word and set up fillable bubbles and other enhancements and made them super-easy for people to use from then on. It was a revelation. The new templates were populatable and easy and user-friendly and seamless. Then I did a training on how to actually use it at a sales kickoff. Making progress!

6sense was still a startup—it only had about 50 employees—and it didn't have an HR department, so, seeing and hearing the mounting frustrations, I took it upon myself to conduct onboardings and teach some of the tools. A lot of employees were new to Office 365, so they had resistance and objections to the apps, and they needed somebody to help them over the hump. I would sit down with each person that came through the door and walk them through an onboarding session, including best practices and use of tools. I'd show them how to use SharePoint, whether they were on a PC or a Mac. Then we decided to scale those one-on-one trainings to include several people—and my trainings expanded.

The more I spoke, led, and trained, the more confident I became. The more I found I could add value. As someone who wanted to just quietly sit behind a computer undisturbed, I became a person who would say "Yes" to public speaking without a second thought. The momentum built on itself and it became what you might call a virtuous circle.

The crazy thing is that it fed something in me that I didn't know I had at the time: an insatiable curiosity to continuously improve myself and my work environment. From workflow to templates to teaching others how to leverage the tools they use every single day, I was making a difference. What started as one-on-one onboardings morphed into trainings for up to 60 people. I taught Word, Excel, PowerPoint, and productivity tools, which helped the individual employees but also helped raise the productivity of the entire company and helped deliver a six-figure ROI at the company that year. It all started to feed off of itself. My confidence grew more, and I felt like I was leveraging the momentum.

Then in 2018, our CRO at the time, Dave Simon, was planning a sales kickoff, and he came up to me and said, "Hey Maggie, why don't you lead a session on PowerPoint enablement for us?" And I thought, *I'd love to*. I was truly excited. The whole thing was sparking my passion like nothing else.

Leadership Mastery

About three years earlier, I had seen *I Am Not Your Guru*, a documentary film focusing on one of Tony Robbins' events, Date with Destiny. It really resonated with me. When I saw that movie, I knew with every fiber of my being that I would find a way to go to that event myself. I didn't know how; I didn't know when; but I knew I would go. Then, when I saw the price tag, I was crestfallen. Now what? So I made the decision that I would find a way to go to Tony's Unleash the Power Within in 2018 instead. And once I did that, I knew I had to go to his Date with Destiny event, too, so I figured out a way to attend that year, too. After that, I signed up for Leadership Mastery and now I'm on track to become a Senior Leader.

Just after I had come back from Date with Destiny, our VP of Sales, Mark Ebert, approached me.

"How was your Tony Robbins event, Maggie?" he asked me.

"Mark, I just came from a hundred hours of training. I don't really know what I can tell you in five minutes. Are you sure you want to open that box right now?"

"You know what?" he said, "You're right. Why don't you lead a session at sales kickoff instead? I don't care what you do—I trust you, just do it."

That 3-Letter Word
So I did.

At our January SKO that year, I led a session of 60 people, alongside four chiefs and a director—and it was the most fulfilling experience of my professional career to date, I have to say. The session was called "Meet the Pros." It started by having each Pro spend 10 minutes talking about what their specialty was, what they were known for around the company, and how they did what they did. It was like speed dating—six tables of 10 people spend 10 minutes at each table, rotating each Pro every 10 minutes over the course of an hour.

Then I went around the room, spending about ten minutes at each table, and I led something I called "Realtime Revelations." I spoke about the power of language. Our language alone can have an incredible impact on the range of our feelings and emotions and can quite literally make the difference between someone living their best life or living a life of pain and suffering. The words we think and speak create our stories. The stories we tell ourselves and others create our behavior, actions, habits, and ultimately our destiny. They shape our reality. I shared that there's a three-letter word that we let impact our lives in a big way. But to see the effect of it, they had to do a little exercise. I asked them to think about something that they want, and then write down whatever it is, whether it's a new car, a new house, a promotion, or whatever. Then I asked them to write down why they *can't* have whatever it is that they want. For example, "I want a new car, but I don't have the money," So everyone wrote that down. Then I had each person read theirs out loud to the others at their table.

When I asked people about their reaction to what they wrote, everyone said that it felt defeating, it felt like shit, or even crippling—like they couldn't progress. I could see it in their body language, too. Their shoulders were hunched over, their bodies were slumped, often times with their head hung low. And then I said, "Okay, so there's a three-letter word in that sentence that's prohibiting you from having what you want." I watched their eyes light up when they realized it was the word "but."

So we talked about it.

"It's just a three-letter word," I continued. "It's just language. But the truth is, 'A' usually has nothing to do with 'B', and yet, you're letting 'B' impact your life. Whether you want to go work out, or you want to join hockey with your son, or you want to buy a Peloton, or whatever it is—all these excuses are holding you back. Now I want you to cross out the word "but" and write the word "and.""

We strive to live a life that's happy, joyous, and free, yet that's nearly impossible. Why not embrace, learn from, and enjoy the journey? You get to decide.

It was the most beautiful thing. I calculated that about 80% of the room had transformations just from that exercise alone. And then I had them go around the table again and read out their sentence again saying "and" instead of "but." Like, "I want to buy a Peloton" and, instead of saying "*but* I can't afford it," saying, "*and* I can't afford it." You could also say "and I can't afford it *right now*," to be even more specific. By doing this, you get to see that one has nothing thing to do with the other. 'B' can't diminish 'A'. If you want a Peloton, then what to do becomes more clear. Stop buying your lattes, don't go shopping, don't go out to the bars, et cetera, and go buy your Peloton. That's what's going to get the excuses out of the way.

When I started talking about this kind of stuff, sharing with people some of the tools I'd learned from the trainings and workshops I'd invested in, I knew that this is what I wanted to be doing. I was on fire.

The Fruits

I continue to deliver trainings, whether it's 1:1, small groups, sales kickoff, Quarterly Business Reviews and the occasional company-wide All Hands on how to leverage the tools that are at our fingertips.

Because I've grown comfortable speaking in public and see how much of a difference I can make, I continue to say Yes to opportunities to speak that come my way. I continue to do employee onboarding trainings on best practices, tips, and benefits, teach how to leverage the tools at our fingertips, and PowerPoint Enablement trainings at our QBRs. I've presented SMART goals in Reflektive in company-wide meetings and was invited by one of our top-producing sales reps to share my personal "Best Of" tips at her goal-setting session at our SKO. And, I've been asked to be a guest on a handful of industry podcasts.

In 2019, I had the honor of speaking with Jason, our CEO, at the Executive Leadership Support (ELS) Forum in front of 150 C-suite EAs. Our talk was titled, "The Intricacies of Forming A Strategic Partnership." Being invited to speak with my CEO felt incredible. I remember being in the audience at a similar event years ago, thinking, "I hope I share the stage with a stellar CEO, too, one day. That'd be pretty sweet!" And there I was, doing just that.

With a certain amount of poetic symmetry, I was also invited to speak at Bonnie Low-Kramen's BTUA event alongside my chief revenue officer just five years after I had so dramatically melted down there. While I hadn't even been able to complete a two-minute presentation my first time around, five years later, Dave Simon and I were surprise guest speakers with a 45-minute talk. I had come full circle. That experience was truly a gift.

And, either ironically, or as a testament to my commitment and the program's effectiveness, last June I received the following email from Peter Khoury, the founder of Magnetic Speaking:

Hi Maggie,

How are you? I have a quick question ☺

Would you consider becoming a part-time trainer with us at Magnetic? I think you would make an awesome trainer and our clients will learn and be inspired by you... Everyone I checked with at Magnetic agrees with me and would love to have you be part of the team.

Peter

You could say I've gone from crash-and-burn to being a force for good. Not too bad for five years' work. I've expanded my reach even further at events beyond the EA realm, getting invited to speak at other events on other topics. It's all incredible for me to witness. It's beyond anything I could have possibly imagined only a few years ago. It's amazing what can happen when you open your mind and heart to what is possible!

When you show up, magic happens.

6
ARE WE WORTH IT?

"Nope—no way. Good luck even trying. Our CFO would never approve it. It's just a boondoggle."

Confused, I replied, "A 'boon'—*what?*"

It was several years ago, and there I was, an assistant to a C-level executive at some company simply asking the senior director of HR to invest in some training and education for me at a highly regarded executive assistant conference that was coming up. They declined my suggestion.

After googling "boondoggle," I felt defeated and dejected once again. My world had been spiraling out of control, I was bored, bored, bored at work, and something needed to change. I was questioning myself all over again.

But something in me persisted. One thing I knew for sure: attending conferences for executive assistants was calling my name loud and clear. That was how I would grow, get better at my job, be more productive, be more responsible, and have a greater impact. But why couldn't this HR director—and most of the other C-level and HR decision-makers around the country—see that my being educated and trained would add to their bottom line, too?

In my experience, administrative professionals are often told, "You do your job just fine. You don't need training. There isn't a budget for that anyway."

Initially, I believed it, and for years I allowed it to impact how I showed up for my job. Wouldn't you? Imagine yourself showing up to the office having just heard, "You don't need training." Your reaction? "They said I don't need training. I guess I don't need training. Hey! I don't need training! Go me!" Then, how do you expect the sentiment would affect you in other ways, like how you respond to requests, interact with people, and show up in general?

I know my reaction was to go into a bit of self-righteous know-it-all-ness. I'd have a "my way or the highway" attitude and get closed, defensive, argumentative, and eventually complacent. Why not? If the status quo was good enough, then I better damn well have all the answers just as I am.

Then there's the ding to the ego—and many of us have egos that are sorely insecure. In my mind at least, the message, "We don't have budget for that," translated into, "They don't value me. I'm not good enough. I'm not worth it. So—what's the point in trying? Or giving it all I've got?" Have these thoughts or something similar ever occurred for you?

Still, whether there's a budgeting issue or not, it's critically important to recognize that one thing has nothing to do with the other. You have to remember how much value you add. Period.

We ask ourselves, who am I to be brilliant, gorgeous, handsome, talented and fabulous? Actually, who are you not to be?"
–Marianne Williamson

We Don't Ask Enough

One of my biggest frustrations—and it has been for years—is with the compensation bands for executive assistants. In most organizations, especially in the larger ones, certain positions have levels while others have compensation bands to set policies and ranges for salaries, bonuses, and other forms of remuneration. Engineers, for example, might get assigned Engineer 1, 2, or 3, and be compensated with salaries and bonuses that increase with advancement. But for some reason, executive assistance compensation is all over the map. Adding insult to injury, EAs don't have a safety net, no golden parachute, receive little to zero equity or RSUs and we're often the lowest compensated professional employees overall, yet working alongside of and impact the output of the highest compensated people in the building.

Making things even more challenging is the fact that, traditionally, EAs have a difficult time communicating their wants and needs. Most of us are fearful of being seen as incompetent, not good enough, or unworthy. (Sound familiar?) We don't want to be rejected, or worse, fired. If we do finally work up the courage to ask for resources, only to get turned down the first time we ask, we usually don't ask again. What results is a vicious cycle and diminishing returns. We take on too much trying to prove our worth, which often leads us to fill up with anger and resentment, and then we bring it home. Eventually it all turns into burnout and we end up looking elsewhere—only to repeat the cycle.

At a few events I've been to, I've been able to conduct informal polls to see what people were experiencing around asking for compensation increases. I told the group that I wanted to get a feel for numbers and asked everyone to please raise their hand if they had asked for a salary increase within the last year or two. In a room full of 150 people, how many hands do I see go up? Not many. Maybe 20%.

Then, to the people with raised hands, I said, "Okay, thank you. Please keep your hands up. Now, once you were told "No" the first time, how many of you asked again?" How many hands do you think stayed up? Very few. The last time I did this in a room full of 150 people, a few hands stayed up, but the time before that, every single hand went down.

As EAs, our tendency to keep our mouths shut and not ask for what we want or need feeds the problem. Our compensation bands stay stuck in the past and get adjusted for *maybe* the cost of living (via cost of living adjustment—COLA) on occasion, but nothing commensurate with the value that we bring to our executives and our organizations. Bottom line? We need to speak up—for ourselves and for each other.

The only obstacle in my life is me. And I'll tell you a secret: that's true for you, too.

Look. To say the obvious, the EAs role is critical to the success of the company. From planning offsites, SKOs and strategy sessions, to connecting people to people and people to information; from supporting top executives in virtually every way—personally and professionally—to noticing and reporting where there are gaps or issues emerging; from connecting the dots between executive travel and reps' opportunities so that deals move forward to keeping our fingers on the pulse of our orgs. When we do our job, we are absolutely essential to the success of our organization. We are the string that ties it together, the buffer zone, the anticipator, the fixer, the listener, and the problem-solver wrapped in one.

Yet since I've become aware of this reality over the last five years, I feel like I've been beating my head against a wall due to the existence of "the data" that tells a single, stagnant, uninformed story about EA performance and value. As much as I appreciate working with Jason, when we start talking about compensation, he goes old school on me and immediately says something to the effect of, "Well, Maggie, it all goes back to the data."

My eyes glaze over. *How can he not see the obvious?*

"But, Jason," I counter, "when you read the data, you are comparing me to hundreds of thousands of other executive assistants—from entry level to director to VP. But we're not all the same. Our job descriptions are not the same, and the value we add to our organizations are not the same. Not all those EAs are sitting in on the leadership meetings and driving the OKRs for their organizations. So your argument about data is irrelevant."

I've started to get his attention on the matter.

I'm trying to view it as an opportunity. While it can be extremely frustrating at times, I'm absolutely committed to carrying the torch if need be, to paving the way, and to working with other influencers in our space to continually shine a light on the value that we bring to our organizations.

The good news is that a few EA influencers, Bonnie included, are speaking up for us in a powerful way. They're part of a task force that is working with the U.S. Labor Bureau to come up with a new band for C-suite EAs. It'll probably take several years to change things, but it will go a long way to help our cause.

We must continue to ask for compensation commensurate with our worth—for ourselves and for everyone that's following in our footsteps.

What's Your Figure?

Before I attended my first BTUA in 2013, Bonnie Low-Kramen had introduced me to Jean Francese, executive/personal assistant and VP of administrative operations at Alibaba Group. Jean is a force and a straight shooter, so when I met her, I took the opportunity to get her thoughts about compensation—and mine in particular. I shared with her my experience, my skillset, and what I deliver, and I asked her what she thought my salary should be based on what I told her. Without a second thought, she blurted out a figure. Now, the figure she gave me was an amount I had never received, much less had the confidence to ask for. It was, of course, during a time where it was perfectly acceptable for a would-be employer to ask, "What are you currently making?" and then offer you compensation based on your personal historical data. Never mind the role you're interviewing for or the extent of your previous contributions. But by having a clear figure in mind that I felt good about, one "blessed" by Jean Francese, it gave me the confidence I needed from then on to ask for a range much higher than I previously made or was currently making. And all it took was her encouragement.

Was it easy to ask for that range the first time? Of course not. But I put one foot in front of the other and with each call screen and interview, I practiced and eventually owned verbalizing that salary range. I discovered that I could test the waters and build my confidence as I did. So, when I was looking for a new position, I took recruiting calls, especially the entry-level ones. They'd tell me about the job, and I'd throw out a salary range that I wanted and see how it was received. The first time I did that, my voice trembled. I could barely get the words out! And they basically laughed at me and hung up. But as I became more confident in my delivery, I was able to get through it and sound credible. I'd hear a variety of responses, everything from, "Oh, that's not in budget," or "Good luck," to "Let me check with our CFO about that." But after a while, they started saying, "Okay, great. We want to bring you in for an interview," or "Yeah, that's fine. When can you come in?" (For what it's worth, do keep in mind that the big companies often end up hiring from within. After taking all that time with you, I've heard and experienced first-hand they frequently hire internally. So, don't get your hopes up too high with them and take a multi-threaded approach when interviewing.)

I was getting emboldened. I refused to stay where I was and remain stagnant, and so I got stronger in my delivery. I'd say, "I'm currently evaluating opportunities between $XXk and $XXXk." And then I'd shut my mouth. No justifying. No reasons why. This is my range. Period. It's one thing if you've not yet found a way to communicate your value, and I admit that I occasionally struggle with that even today. But it's quite another if someone else is unable to see the value you deliver after you clearly articulate where you've been and where you're going. Thanks to my little heart-to-heart with Jean, I increased my salary by 40% at my next job. Know your value so you can speak your value.

But you have to be assertive. Most executives I've had the privilege of meeting are brilliant and remarkable in their own right. Many are truly compassionate, empathetic, and genuinely want to see those they work with succeed in their role and beyond. So, while you debate and think about how to ask your executive to invest in you, ask yourself a different question, "Why *wouldn't* he or she want to invest in me?" You have this person's back, their best interest in mind, you help them strike a balance between their work and home life, you connect dots, you build bridges, and you gently remind them of things they may otherwise have forgotten. You help ensure that their brand remains the same—within the organization and external to it—or even expands, as it did when they first took the role.

I look forward to the day where my compensation is either a percentage of my executive's in some form or another and/or it is in alignment with the impact I have on his success vs. measured against current, stagnant data sets. My work is an extension of his work; working with high-level EAs enables our executives to deliver at the levels that they do. We're force multipliers and should be compensated accordingly.

People often ask me why I think it's a company's responsibility to pay for trainings. My response is that it's not their responsibility—but if you have a company that pays for and invests in coaches for the chiefs and VPs, why would you not want to train your EAs as well? They are an extension of the executives. I answer the question by asking the question differently. In the next chapter, I'll share with you some helpful strategies for having a conversation with your exec about compensation.

In the meantime, here are a few things I recommend you include when negotiating your next role working with a CEO:

- Stock options commensurate with a VP-level title. Be bold. Ask. Do it. Household names you and I both know have successfully asked and received.

- Choice of title, such as Director, Executive Administration; Director, Executive Operations, VP, Business Administration; Chief of Staff; etc.

- $5k *quarterly* training budget plus tuition reimbursement, or an MBA, if that's your calling

- 30% minimum bonus. Ask for more initially, with the majority tied to personal performance vs. company performance

- Consistent access to coaching for you *and* your executive

- Executives get a golden parachute. A silver one for us would be nice. It would take me a minimum of three months to find another job, and six months is probably more realistic.

Disclosure: these are big asks. If you get all of them, hats off to you! If you get a fraction of any one of them, be grateful. We've come a long way, and yet we still have a long way to go.

You are working alongside the highest compensated people in the building. You're an extension of them—why shouldn't that be partially reflected in your compensation and your career path for growth and training? You function as a force multiplier, enabling them to function at a higher level than they would without you. Remember that.

Invest in You

Regardless of your money story, it's important to remember to choose and commit to investing in yourself—invest with your time, your energy, your attention, and your money. It's that simple. When you choose and commit to investing in yourself and your own personal and professional growth every quarter, every year, transformation occurs. It's that simple.

And while I encourage you to ask for reimbursement for training and personal development, I also would say that you shouldn't let that drive your decisions. Don't shortchange yourself and your future based on what your company will or won't do for training budget. Your potential ROI in personal and professional growth is infinite. We really have no idea what we are capable of creating in our lifetimes!

If you won't invest in you, why should your company invest in you?
—Lauren Hasson, Founder,
Develop[Her]

7
THE ELEVATED EA

Like many things in life, the role of an EA is really what you make of it. But I also believe, and have personally discovered, that we EAs are in the enviable position of interacting with some of the world's most inspiring influencers and operating at some of the highest echelons of industry—so the truism is especially true for us. We help make things happen for powerful people, usually with efficiency, prescience, and precision. When asked to define the job of an executive assistant in one sentence, I like to say: "I work in the space of 'executive enablement'— I make things possible for my executive," because we are in the unique position to fulfill on limitless possibilities.

Yes, I truly believe we can create the role of our dreams, if we choose to do so.

How do you do that? The first step is to consider reinventing your mission to be something along the lines of what Robin Guido voiced: *"My role is to help my executive reach their next level."* Recalibrating your role this way can change virtually everything by changing your focus. The change of perspective will pull you out of self-centered entitlement—which people can get so lost in today, myself included at times. Instead, you begin to look for ways you can add value and deliver at the highest level. This adjustment—elevating our role in this way—can literally change everything. It did for me.

The next step is to look for what's broken and take it upon yourself to take steps to fix it. When people ask me, "Where do I start?" I ask them, "What frustrates you?" The keys to the kingdom are in finding what's broken, what's not working, what people bitch and complain about—whatever frustrates you the most, whether it's a system or a process, whatever it is— go fix it. Go plug that hole, go bridge that gap, go make that connection.

It can be incredibly satisfying.

You are not your thoughts, your stories, your limiting beliefs. You are capable of being anyone and anything you can dream of.

Getting my Microsoft Office Specialist certification opened my eyes about this. Once I had those tools under my belt, I found myself with a passion for finding what needed to be fixed—and fixing it. And so, every template, every form, every deck that malfunctioned, every time I became frustrated with something specific to Microsoft— because let's face it, there are a lot of frustrations—I would raise my hand and say, "Let me build that." Or, "Let me create that." "Let me show you how to do this. Let me show you how to format a 50-page document in less than five minutes."

Our sales teams were using incredibly janky proposal templates that weren't properly created in Word, and people were taking a crazy amount of time to reformat each paragraph before sending them out. So, I took it upon myself to right the ship. I recreated a fillable form that we could scale and use across the sales org. I created something that works, and it has become a win for everyone that uses it.

We were using Reflektive, a useful internal review app, but I noticed that it was being underutilized. It has a great real-time feedback feature that integrates with Slack, which the company uses for internal messaging. And so anytime someone does something great, anyone can offer real-time feedback and say, "Way to Go!" or "That was great!" or "Killer presentation with Customer XYZ!" — and the entire company gets to see the feedback, including managers. And then, when it's performance review time, and you're sitting there scratching your head wondering what you had accomplished over the past period, you can go and look at all the feedback you've received. Everyone loves it! They thank each other, they love to be acknowledged publicly, and they get the visibility with the executive team. It creates an incredible virtuous circle. It took me a year and a half to get it put in play, but it was worth it. In the early roll-out phase, I had to remind the executives, day in, day out, to use it, since I knew I had to start at the top if things were going to get rolling. And now, most everyone uses it. It's a well-oiled machine. It's beautiful!

That's how you add value. Find something that isn't working. Think about all those things that you complain about or that you have a constant inner dialogue with yourself about that "this doesn't work" or "I wish we had this; I wish we had that." Go out and build it. Don't wait to be asked. Don't wait for somebody to come in and do it. Be that person. You have that power.

> ## *We get what we tolerate.*
> ## *–Tony Robbins*

Think about it. What frustrates you? What process is lacking or doesn't yet exist? What bugs the shit out of you or frustrates you to no end? What is the bane of your existence? Listen to that, tap into it, and instead of asking, "Can anyone do anything around here?" ask, "What can I do to create a seamless process around this?" Being a problem-solver like this can help you deliver tremendous value to your company, and it can also transform your perception of yourself. You're no longer a victim of your surroundings. You can get things done.

Questions to Open Possibilities

The questions you ask yourself each day can drive the direction of your work, your vision, and your self-esteem. They drive your thoughts, your actions, and your habits—which shape your destiny.

If you change your questions, you change your life. So, think about what questions you ask yourself each day. If you're not getting the answer you want, change your question! Most people ask themselves disempowering questions like, "What's wrong with me?" "What's wrong with them?" "How can I fix this?" "How can I get them to like me?" "What's the point?" "Is this all there is?" "Why me?" "How come I can't...?"

Here are some more empowering questions to ask yourself. Take some time with them. Sit down and write out your answers and be as honest with yourself as you can. Really give them some thought; dig deep. If you find it uncomfortable, don't get spooked; lean into the discomfort and see what shows up for you. They will inevitably help you see things that are keeping you stuck and ways that you are limiting yourself.

- *Am I living in the past or future?*

- *Am I asking myself empowering or disempowering questions?*

- *What stories am I telling myself?*

- *Where am I stuck?*

- *Who am I blaming?*

- *Who am I making wrong?*

- *What am I holding on to or unwilling to let go of?*

- *What would happen if I let go of the need to be right?*

- *What would happen if I let go of those stories? What would my life look like?*

- *What do I need to do to let go of those stories?*

- *Who do I need to be(come)?*

- *What's great about this?*

- *What's beautiful about this?*

- *What can I appreciate about this?*

Trade your expectation for appreciation.
No matter what, enjoy the process!
–Tony Robbins

8
MANAGING UP

So, to help embolden you to speak up and speak more often, I want to share with you some insights I've gained from my trainings as well as my own experience. The question is, how do you speak powerfully to your own boss? How do you articulate your value and actually influence how they see you, your job, your contribution, and in fact, the EA work you do?

One of the most powerful conversations I've ever had about the subject was with Phoenix Normand, author and chief at trībU. He gave me a powerful framework that has helped me get more traction in my conversations with my exec than ever by far. His fundamental suggestion was this: when you speak to your CEO, speak to their role. Consider who they are in the many facets of their role, including everything they do to bring a product to life. From product inception and going to market to assembling a world-class team and establishing a raving fan customer base to IPOs and mergers and acquisitions.

I did this for Jason a while ago, breaking down the conversation in a simple table. He was sitting across from me, and I slid the sheet across the desk. He looked it over and said, "Okay. Cool. Now that we're clear on this, ... you can run the company."

"Sure, Dude," I said. We laughed. But that little table simplified everything so elegantly. It gave me the basis to speak to how and what's possible for Jason because I had mapped out, for every aspect of his role, what I can do to help facilitate it. Here's what he can do and here's how I can help him. It made a big impact on many of our subsequent conversations.

Until it didn't. I still have to consistently remind Jason and others of the value I bring. If we don't keep reminding them, they often assume things just "magically happen." People (including me) easily forget how much time and energy it takes to nearly flawlessly execute an event, program, or whatever. So it's important for us to remind them—however casually or formally—of our efforts and the impact of said efforts.

Still, if you speak their language and convey that you grasp the breadth and depth of their job, it gets you in the room. Then, you can help them see your job through the context of the vision and values they have. For example, instead of trying to convince your manager that you need more money and your rent is high, or whatever other reasons you have to get a raise, frame the conversation around what's in it for *them*. How does your work serve their goals? How are you helping them accomplish their vision? Doesn't matter if it's an interview situation or a review, you need to clearly convey that. Make it personal. As Dale Carnegie, author of *How to Win Friends and Influence People,* said, people care more about a boil on their neck than 40 earthquakes in Japan.

When I talk to Jason, I turn the tables around and ask him whether or not he's owning the objectives and key results (OKRs) process. I can be feisty and direct—if you haven't noticed!—so I'll ask him, tongue in cheek, "Who's owning that process? Are you following up with each team and person? What tools are you using?" Part of his role is to assemble a world-class team. Not be in the weeds tracking specifics. So who owns it? Me. He casts the vision, sets the strategy, assembles the team, leads the troops. I connect dots, bridge gaps, and streamline stuff to help him actualize his vision. I remind him of that in a way that points out how much a pain all that kind of stuff is to him. Logistics, systems, and processes are the domains I thrive in, so I speak to the pain that he doesn't want and remind him that by having me owning—or at least driving and tracking—all of it for him, he's freed up to do all those things that he's so good at—focusing on the bigger vision, the strategy, etc. He's the face and voice. He orchestrates. I execute behind the scenes. He's strategy. A to Z. I'm tactics. A to B. B to C. C to D. You get the picture.

Getting Heard

In January 2018, as I was walking out the door after my review, I literally turned on my heels and spontaneously made my first "big" ask. It was something I felt strongly about, and it was at a time when I was starting to get an inkling that it's my responsibility to own my future.

"I'm going to kick myself if I don't ask," I said, which was true. "Will you please support me in attending this?" It was a Tony Robbins event I was very drawn to going to. I'd already asked for the time off, and I had already paid for it. But I thought, *You know what? This* is *training and development. Why not ask?* So I did.

He didn't blink, hardly looked up, and said, "Yes. Now, is there anything else?"

Get in their head by speaking their language, using their terms, embracing their mindset. Read what they read. Listen to what they listen to. Ask, "What podcasts do you listen to? What books are you reading?" instead of, "Why can't we have better swag or snacks?" Sprinkle in words like "ROI" and "profit and loss" and "retention" and "bottom line." You've got to talk about things through their lens: morale, attracting and retaining talent, customer retention, and how to accomplish the company's quarterly and annual goals.

> *Let's talk about what's possible, your role, and how I can help you get you to where you want to be.*

To have powerful, bilateral conversations with your executive, you have to embrace their perspective, and put yourself in their shoes. Okay, so maybe they are lost in the data related to your comp, maybe benchmarks are shit or outdated, or aren't commensurate with today, your value, and your impact. But you also have to respect and appreciate (I didn't say agree) that they are trying to make sense of the story that the data is telling them. They usually make their decisions based on data, so the rational does make sense. So, say that. "I appreciate and respect where you're coming from and your perspective on the data. Let me share with you the impact and ROI that your hiring me (or an increase in compensation, an investment in training, etc.) will do for the company. And if we work well together long-term, let me tell you about what and how I'll contribute to your brand and professional trajectory."

Now, if you have some specific and measurable numbers to share, share them! If you have real numbers about the amount of time that was saved across the organization due to your work, and what that translates to in terms of dollars, you'll get their attention. Then you can speak to what's possible in their future.

Here's one of my favorite examples. Let's say you deliver a 30-minute PowerPoint enablement training session, and, for simplicity's sake, you've got ten attendees. Now, how many of them have wasted more than 10 minutes formatting a PowerPoint slide? And how much money is being wasted because they do that? Let's do the numbers. Ten attendees. An average deck is ten slides. Ten minutes per slide, multiplied by their base salary. Now it gets even more interesting. Let's say they make three decks a week, so you want to multiply that last number by 4.2, the number of weeks in a month, and, while you're at it, calculate it with the number of weeks in a year, or 52.

The last time I did this—and I presented it in an Excel doc—that final number amounted to more than $400,000. Four hundred thousand dollars was actually going down the drain due to lack of training—or better said—I had saved the company $400k with my training. When you put the numbers together like that for them, you can say, "Mr. CEO, I delivered a 30-minute PowerPoint enablement training session and saved the company over $400,000—but that's just calculated on their base salary. Let me plug in their on-target earnings number (OTE), too, and then the savings increases to over $750,000." Make sense?

That's one of favorite ways to ask for more money or to show my exec their *real* return on investment (ROI)—in me. It makes them stop and think. They are impressed and you can see the wheels start to turn in their heads.

I can be relentless at times. And it pays off. At the end of 2017, I decided to map out every event in 2018 that I wanted to attend—and there were a lot of them. I put all of them in an Excel spreadsheet, including the cost of each one and the grand total for all of them put together, including airfare and hotel. Go big or go home. When it was time for my one-on-one with Jason, I sauntered on up to his desk and slid it across the table for him to take a look at.

He moved his hand to cover his mouth. I could tell he was trying not to laugh in front of me.

"What is this?" he asked casually.

"Oh, these are all the events that I'd like to attend next year," I said trying to mirror his casualness.

"Um, well, you can have the *time*..." He looked at it again. The total cost for all the trainings and T&E amounted to over $20,000.

"Maggie, even *I* don't get $20k in training."

"Okay."

"But we are going to think about expanding our learning and development policy."

I said, "Okay, great. Thank you. I'll be back."

He said, "I know you will!"

Then, every few months I'd bring it up again in my one-on-ones. In the meantime, I'd send him emails I'd gotten from the various events I'd been to—the ones that beckoned, saying only a hundred tickets remained, and that sort of thing. But then I remembered Lauren Hasson of DevelopHer asking me: "If you won't invest in yourself, why should your company invest in you?" And that really resonated with me. I've heard so many EAs say, "Well, if my company won't pay for it, I'm not going." But that strikes me as a terribly self-defeating mindset. It's a stagnant mindset, really. You can't let your company dictate your success. So, I took a different approach. I decided that I'm committed to investing in myself, so if an executive or company (Jason, in this case) chose not to invest me and my training, that's ok. It's likely indicative of our longevity together. I decided I was going to become a *beast* of an EA, and if he wanted to work together with me, great. If not, that's cool, too. Somebody else will.

> *In the final analysis, the one quality that all successful people have is the ability to take on responsibility.*
> *–Michael Korda, editor-in-chief,*
> *Simon & Schuster*

From that, I made the decision that I was going to go to all of the events that I wanted to go to, on my own dime. Long gone was the mentality of, "I'll attend, but only if the company pays for it." I'm committed to *me*. And yet, focused on growth for the greater good, every few months I would go back to him and ask, "So! How's that training and development policy coming along?" I'd keep it all very nonchalant, very tongue-in-cheek, and he wouldn't have an answer. But I kept asking even so. And every so often I'd get a "Yes." And by the end of the year, I had gone to every single event on that list, events that have enriched me both personally and professionally beyond measure. In the meantime, I was reimbursed for almost half of my personal outlay that year —partly because I asked and asked and asked and partly because I showed my passion for being great at what I do. And to think I was almost too scared to ask!

I share this not to impress you but to impress upon you that we *must* advocate for ourselves. No one else is thinking about you, your growth, or your career trajectory to the level that you should and must be. This is about *you*.

Step up. Show Up. Ask. Grow. Reflect and repeat.

You don't get if you don't ask. ASK. Always.

If you focus on goals, you may hit goals-but that doesn't always guarantee growth. If you focus on growth, you will grow and always hit goals.
-John C. Maxwell

Getting on the Same Page

Believe it or not, conversations around compensation have historically rattled me to my core. And they occasionally still do—more than I care to admit. It doesn't actually matter whether somebody wants to talk to me about business decisions, benchmarks of current industry standards, or my perception of the value of the contributions I've made, conversations around remuneration make me crazy. I think it's because of how I was raised. In fact, I've spent countless hours doing internal work, processing my emotions that come up about money.

For over a year and a half, I had been carrying anger and resentment towards Jason because of a promise he had made early on about my work—a promise he did not keep. And finally, after all that time, I sat him down and shared with him how I had been affected. When I did, I felt incredibly free. My goal was to restore my sanity and protect the integrity of the relationship. I wasn't expecting anything to change, and it wasn't really the time for that discussion. But after that, we scheduled another meeting. The topic: recalibration and revisiting expectations about my role.

Just one day before this exchange, he had shared with the executive team that he felt that the senior execs should take immense care to go the extra mile for the people that work for them. They should have their back, knowing how much the other impacts their lives and their work. Naturally, I was skeptical.

When we met again, Jason wanted to review the main points of the issue one more time. As he walked through the timelines of 2017 and 2018 and what had occurred with the incremental pay increases, my eyes glazed over. I could feel myself quickly shutting down and checking out from the conversation. *Here we go again. I'm so over it… Fuuuuck this,* I thought. Old behaviors die hard. But then I caught myself.

"Jason," I stopped him. "I appreciate you wanting to review this—the data, the timelines—with me again. Really, I do. But I can't. Let's move on. Please." I didn't need an apology; I needed him to see how his actions (or lack thereof) had had a detrimental effect on me and my work. Instead of running the internal dialogue in my head (of which he had no idea), I shared my thoughts and that was enough. I realized that I had been holding on to something for months on end, and that it was up to me to reveal it in order to heal it. Sure, I might have some frustrations and tinges of resentment here and there from time to time, but I began to see that it wasn't doing me any good holding on to that stuff. While it might be human nature, it's a waste of internal real estate. It wasn't serving me. Also, all of it had *nothing* to do with him and everything to do with stuff in my past. What's that quote? "Holding on to anger and resentment is like drinking poison and expecting the other person to die." It's a waste of time.

Now was the time to refocus on the future.

So, I posed a question. "Tell me, when do you want to retire?" (See how I pivoted the conversation to be about *his* goals?)

He looked at me, spending a beat deep in thought. "Um, 57."

"Okay, so we've both expressed an interest in working together for the long term. But with how things transpired, how could I not have reacted the way I did? It has nothing to do with the money and everything to do with the larger picture—with who I can be and what I can do for you, the company, and your future endeavors beyond 6sense."

I asked him to step into the future. "I'd like to invite you into a new world of possibilities, one where, perhaps, my compensation is aligned with yours and based on the value I add to the organization."

"Let's talk about your role. (Because my role is to help him reach his next level, remember?) As CEO, your role is to transform a concept into a must-have product, then assemble a dream team to build, sell, and evolve the product, then create and nurture industry connections, then turn customers into evangelists, then make money and build your own credibility, and finally, sell, IPO, and move on to our next play." I drew from the Excel list I had built before.

Remember that first meeting I had with Jason on a Sunday, when I arrived with a deck and a book to talk about what's possible? The response I got this conversation was virtually the same. His eyes lit up.

From there, the ideas flowed. We talked about the future—what he wants, the steps we need to take to get there, and where we go from here. It was entirely future-focused; the past was behind us. Now we were aligned once again, and maybe better than ever.

Redirecting your conversations with your executive towards their vision, their plans, their values, and needs can finally get their attention, get you on the same page, and help you do your job even better. And in those moments of frustration, disappointment, feelings of failure—whatever it may be—talk about it. Communicate. They aren't mind readers…in fact, far from it. We're supposed to be the mind readers. Growth comes in many forms, including those conversations that aren't easy or comfortable.

9
YOU'RE NOT ALONE

I meet EAs and PAs all the time that have 10, 20, even 30 years on me. Some are married, but many are single or divorced. And for several years, I too, lived an insular, single life and spent a lot of time involved in things that helped me avoid connecting with people. My driving doctrines were "I got this," and "I don't need anyone." So my life was little more than work-work-work, and I expected that that would never change. I relentlessly pursued professional development and training because—I can see now—it gave me a false sense of security in the belief that I might make myself indispensable to the organization. But at what cost? Even my marriage was at risk at one point. Who knew there can be too much of a good thing? "I'm going to end up alone," I told myself, "so what's the point in trying to nurture a relationship, anyhow?"

Sound familiar? Maybe, maybe not.

If you're at a smaller company, as I am, it's easy to feel all alone, particularly if you're supporting top-tier chiefs or the CEO. Some of us work "on an island"—maybe you're the only EA in your office, or you aren't part of a larger admin team. I've been there. People from all over come to you with information that they might or might not want filtered up. So you're the gateway, and that can be extremely isolating on top of everything else.

But the truth is, relationships are everything, whether it be romantic relationships, personal relationships, or professional relationships. While it might be common for many of us to isolate ourselves in order to get our work done, we don't have to feel alone. Connecting and reaching out to others can fuel your growth, inspire new directions, and make life more joyful and meaningful. You'll be surprised at how much stepping outside of your comfort zone and taking time to network with people—those in your circles and those outside of them—will add to your quality and richness of life and your value on the job.

Businesses are based on relationships. Relationships are formed by people. Most of the best leaders have incredible people skills, and they cultivate and nurture their relationships. So, again, be sure to connect with people, because at the end of the day, we're all just people looking to connect with, to feel seen, heard, acknow ledged and appreciated by other people. I know that I would not be where I am today without the support, guidance, insight, feedback, and encouragement of many people who I've taken the time to engage with, share with, get real with, and learn from. So whether you're an extrovert by nature or a hardcore introvert, you do your future self a disservice by not networking. You just have to do it.

As for your work, trust me, it will still be there when you return. Your inbox isn't going anywhere. There will always be one more thing to do, one more "to do" for your To Do list. It's just that there's more to life. Think of it this way: to play at the next level, we must pay at the next level. You're not going to reach your goals simply by reading a book.

Secrets to Success

One way to expand out and open to new opportunities is to immerse yourself in the content that you're interested in, whether it's signing up for courses, reading books, attending events, getting connected with the people at events, or up leveling your peer group. Who are you hanging out with? Who are you spending time with? Are they contributing to your goals in the future that you want? Are they subtracting? There's no reason to wallow in isolation since there are so many choices that will nurture your growth.

> *You're not going to become the person that you want to become by sitting in your current role doing nothing.*

And there are so many ways to connect—forums, events, and many other resources that we have access to. There's Facebook groups that are free and Slack memberships where you can pay to join. There's an EA group with 10k+ members on Facebook—you might go into it to learn, or you might go into it asking, "What can I give?" If you have 20+ years of experience, you probably have a lot to share that others could learn from.

Think of it this way: networking and connecting are not only good for your soul, they're crucial to your success. Interacting with people challenges you, gives you a sense of camaraderie, and offers you sounding boards for your ideas and assumptions. When you connect up with others and you feel safe enough, you can even share about your failures—we all have them, and if you say you don't, you're either being dishonest with everyone or yourself—and even more importantly, celebrate your wins.

I'm currently a member of a Slack group with some high level EAs, and we get on there and we support and encourage each other. We answer each other's questions and listen to each other's concerns. My favorite is the Wins channel, where we share and celebrate each other's successes. It's valuable to my own growth and to all the other members of the channel.

When you meet people, you never know how that connection will grow and unfold in the future. Remember the difference that crossing paths with Robin Guido made in my life? After reaching out to her, I later ended up having one of the biggest job interviews in my life, and it led to the germination of some invaluable contacts. And to think that I initially didn't want to interview at Salesforce because it was *too big*. But if I hadn't introduced myself, she never would have, a year and a half later, tapped me to interview for a job I never would have applied for in the first place. When we make connections, we have no idea where they can lead. But it's a no-brainer that if you don't reach out, nothing will result from it.

Especially as EAs, I think these days it has become absolutely critical to become part of the EA community. It's essential to our role now because, within just the past five to ten years, EA influencers have really stepped up and shared their vision, their tools, their lessons of empowerment. People like Bonnie Low-Kramen, Vickie Sokol Evans, Al-Husein Madhany, Phoenix Normand, and Jeremy Burrows. There's a wealth of coaching out there to help you step up your game and feel more satisfied and comfortable in your career.

Get out and attend workshops, too, and leverage the opportunities that come your way. Consider that attending workshops— particularly on your own dime—isn't just about taking a "day out of the office." It can be an opportunity to significantly alter the trajectory of your path and gain new skills for your work and possibly even a new, more fulfilled, perception of yourself.

Limitations Be Damned

During the Q & A session of an Executive Leadership Support Forum in San Francisco I was attending, a gentleman stood up to share some fascinating facts about the work of an EA. In just three minutes, he ignited a fire in the entire room with words I'll never forget.

"When women read a job description," he said, "they'll see that they hit 'only' nine out of the ten requirements, and they'll ask themselves, 'Am I qualified?' Doubting themselves, they won't apply. Men will see that they meet *one* out of ten of the requirements—and they *will* apply. Men lead with confidence. Women are a hell of a lot more competent than they project, yet they lack confidence. I make more than you. How do I know this? Because I ask. I negotiate. You don't—and HR professionals expect this."

Who is this guy?!? It was the first time I'd heard Al-Husein Madhany, a motivational speaker, coach, and salary negotiator—and I have to say, someone who is truly a gift to the EA community.

His point at this event? To drive home the fact that the reason

C-level EA at Whatever, Inc. make $280k to $320k—and we EAs don't—is because they're putting in for their overtime. "You are not putting in for your time, and it's affecting us all," he said. It shook me to my core.

Let's take a look. At larger companies, most EAs are paid hourly. Yet, while most of us work more than 40 hours, most don't put in for that time. Why not? Several reasons. One: it needs to be approved, which is bullshit. Two: for some reason people think their work should get finished within a predetermined amount of time— which is generally impossible. But still, they feel "less than" for not accomplishing what's expected within that time. Three: they don't want to call attention to the additional time they spent! It's insane. The work might require 50% more time, but they're not getting paid for it.

I really wanted to thank Al-Husein for sharing his insights at that event. When he was speaking, I was standing next to Bonnie in the back of the room, and when he finished, he quickly walked to the back to chat with Bonnie. Now I might be fairly ballsy at times, but I'm also naturally introverted. So there I stood, like a dolt, for ten minutes, next to this charismatic, accomplished lightning rod after he'd had the mic—and I didn't say anything. Nothing! I didn't introduce myself or say Hi or Thank you. Nada. And I regretted it for almost a year and a half.

Do not let that inner voice keep you from doing things that may seem uncomfortable. You have no idea how much it's limiting your future.

Then, as the new year approached, I decided to make a list of influencers within the EA community who I wanted to meet, connect with, and possibly ask to coach me. My goal was to up-level myself. Can you guess who was at the top of the list? Al-Husein Madhany.

I distinctly remember being on some flight when I was making my list. As soon as I was happy with it, I got to work to learn everything I could about everyone on the list. Their background, education, social activity, articles they'd written—whatever LinkedIn and Google offered, I would soak it all up like a sponge.

What I found out about Al-Husein gave me a sinking feeling. Apparently, he was an Emmy-nominated, award-winning documentary film producer, a published author, Georgetown professor, and a Harvard grad with advanced degrees. And I was going to reach out to him? *Why would he want anything to do with me? What value could I possibly bring to him?* I asked myself. But something in me persisted. I *had* to connect with him. I'd find him on LinkedIn and send him a note.

So I searched. And I searched. And I searched. But Al-Husein Madhany wasn't on LinkedIn. Or, if he was, he was so private that I couldn't find him. My gut told me it was the former. Eventually, I gave up, thinking, *Who isn't on LinkedIn? Who is this guy, anyway?* I stalked him on Angel List and Facebook for a while but gave up shortly thereafter. He speaks globally, so I kept an eye out for his name at some of my favorite events. I'd meet him some day. I just knew it.

Eighteen months later, that day arrived. Al-Husein was slated to be on the agenda at Executive Secretary Live in San Jose, which I wanted to attend. I knew with every fiber in my being I needed to be at the event. I couldn't let this opportunity slip by. This was my chance to meet this enigmatic and powerful figure. It's my life and my training, and since I lost out on my first opportunity, I couldn't let that happen again.

But I'd exhausted my training budget. Emails from ESL kept coming, counting off the dwindling number of tickets left before all were sold out… "Just 75 tickets remain! Only 50 tickets left! Get yours now!"

So I did. I ignored the gap in my training budget and paid $1,800 out of pocket to attend an event because Al-Husein was on the agenda. And he delivered. He shared strategies and offered a framework so executive assistants can have a productive compensation conversation in the same language as their executive. Like Phoenix Normand, he advised that we speak in terms of ROI and our impact on our organization and the business as a whole. Since seeing Al-Husein that year, I believe my ROI has multiplied by more than ten times—and this is only the beginning!

His talk electrified me, and I wanted to connect with him. He had shown up at another conference two months before the ESL, and when I saw him, I made a beeline for him so I could introduce myself. And he wasn't on LinkedIn? This huge influencer spoke globally at many well-known EA events, but he wasn't on the most-connected professional network? Come on.

For the next month, I semi-harassed him on Facebook about not having a LinkedIn profile. Every Saturday morning, I'd send him a long message and tell him that he was doing the rest of us a disservice by not being on LinkedIn. I told him I thought that he needed to be more available to the professional community that way. I even offered to build his profile for him if he wanted me to. He eventually built it—finally—and we became friends.

So here's the thing. When you're at events and you listen to speakers share their knowledge and wisdom, or even if they're in the audience and not the one on the stage, do yourself a favor and go introduce yourself. We get stuck in our minds and our perceptions sometimes. If you're like me, your head spins with: "I don't really have anything valuable to say. Nothing to contribute, really." Well, even if that's true for you, go up and say Hello anyway. At least thank them for what they said or the impact that they have had on you. If they left you moved, touched, or inspired, it is your responsibility to thank them. Thank them for the gift they gave you and thank them so that they will continue to move, touch, and inspire others. They immensely appreciate the validation, the acknowledgement—in fact, it fuels them to keep producing and creating. They want to know that their message landed. So just go talk to them and explore your connection with them because you never know where that relationship might lead in the future.

Finally, if you have people in the community that you enjoy and who's message resonates with you, do what I did and make a list of people who inspire you. Then push yourself, reach out to them—but do so in a way that adds value to them. *Not* one that sucks up their time, "Hey can I pick your brain about XYZ." No. How can you serve *them*? You'll be amazed at how little things like that can come back in positive repercussions later.

Nurture your Network

As my executive assistant career progresses, I end up receiving more and more inbound messages from recruiters. And while these days I'm seldom interested in the roles that are presented to me, I usually take the calls anyway. After all, there's a human being on the other side of that message, and I feel compelled to reply to them. This approach has done several things for me: it has allowed me to polish my story, enabled me to go out with recruiters to small communities across multiple industries, and it's helped me learn about what opportunities are out there. On top of all that, I find it just plain character-building for me as I show up for myself and for others. It's also helped me cultivate an image of professionalism, reliability, and integrity, and that pays off.

Simply put, it pays to nurture your network and answer virtually all of those recruiting calls that wind their way to your inbox. Don't let them just come and go; make a point of following up on emerging opportunities. Of course, many of them are not for me. You'll get notices about entry-level contract positions, temp to perm openings, out-on-leave opportunities, and all sorts of other things you might not have any interest in. A lot of people might blow those off, but I don't. After all, recruiters often don't stay in the same role for 15 or 20 years —unless they're the founder of the company, of course. Yet recruiters can sometimes really get who you are and then remember you for openings that cross their desks. In some ways, they're the lifeblood of opportunities in the professional world. And, while those high-level jobs might be posted publicly, they're usually filled from your own network. Your own backyard, you could say. So, it serves you to make sure you respond to the recruiters who reach out to you. You never know what might materialize from a conversation or an interview—today, tomorrow, or years down the road. My willingness to interview at Salesforce, for example, opened up many doors for me and ultimately led to the job I now enjoy at 6sense.

Set your life on fire. Seek those who fan your flames.
—Rumi

Responding to all those calls has also been validating and helped me build my confidence, too. I thought, *Whoa, am I really qualified for this position?* Yet I advanced far along in the interview process.

On a phone call with Robin Guido, I mentioned to her that I make it a point to respond to everyone that reaches out to me. "That's what sets you and me apart." she said, "We respond to everything, regardless of what it is." Of course, I was thrilled that she considered me in her company in that way. But it reinforces that it just doesn't matter if it's a job supporting an entry level role or if it's a position supporting the president, you respond no matter what. And that's I why decided to make that more of an intentional practice, because, after all, everyone on the other side of that computer screen is a human being.

However, that doesn't keep me from streamlining my approach to save me time and headache. I've created a keyboard shortcut to reply to LinkedIn queries that I can use while in the app on my phone. I just type the letters "ln" and this pops up ready to go:

Hi (First name inserted here),

Great to meet you via LinkedIn. Sounds like an exciting opportunity.

Managing expectations, I adore my current team and want to be mindful of your time. I'm certainly happy to connect, chat, and learn more about the role to see if anyone I know may be of interest. Sound good?

If so, please let me know if there's a time in here that works for you: Thank you.

Cheers,
Maggie Jacobs

Beyond recruiters, it's wise to cultivate your network of connections on all levels, including the EA community. You may wind up working for somebody that you interviewed with several years back as a junior EA, or someone you blew off, or someone you were rude to on an email, or someone you didn't respond to. You don't want to regret having turned your back on a perfectly decent human being and find you have to make up for it later.

So, put yourself out there. Have a social media presence—particularly on LinkedIn. Follow people that inspire you. Comment on their content, engage with them, and share their articles and posts with your network. Tag the people when you comment on their posts or share their content. That way, you'll cultivate your own voice that might move or inspire others. You never know who might be watching or listening.

The most incredible opportunities have come from things I could never have imagined.

Say Yes and Then Say Yes Again

It was solely due to relationships that I had cultivated that a recruiter reached out to me and had me interview at Unison. Once again, I wasn't really looking to jump ship at the time, but he contacted me and asked me to send him my resume. So, I did. And then I went to my yoga class. When I got out of yoga, I saw that I had a message from him, telling me that the CEO wanted to meet me the next day. "Can you come in?" he asked. I really didn't know much about the company or the position at all. Still, I said, "Sure."

I met with the CEO on a Friday night, thinking we'd spend about 15 minutes, but I ended up staying for almost 45. "Can you come back next week?" he wanted to know. And again, I wasn't looking, but I just kept saying, "Yes." When we met the next time, he got more direct. "I'm really enjoying the conversation," he admitted. "I could see this happening. But tell me—why would you leave your current role?"

And again, I wasn't looking, so I didn't lead with some BS story. I was honest with him about what was working and what wasn't working for me, although I didn't reveal any details. I told him I was feeling misaligned with my CEO, and I shared my frustration around the compensation as well as some of the ways in which the company did not deliver on their promises. So this guy said to me—and I have to say that I will be eternally grateful that he did—"Regardless if we decide to move forward, Maggie, I'd like you to have that conversation with your CEO because I think it'll be impactful to your relationship with him and your future endeavors."

So this guy, who I was talking to only because I had decided to follow through on opportunities that came my way, is actually the reason that I ended up having that important conversation with Jason that finally cleared the air and allowed us to align more powerfully than ever.

Saying "Yes" has allowed me to pursue numerous opportunities and talk to countless people. I've interviewed with CEOs, COOs, CPOs, and conversed with many founders and recruiters. And in the process, I've learned more about myself, more about the culture, the industry, and the players. I've validated my direction and my passion. I've said "Yes" to build and nurture my network and to see if there are additional opportunities out there for me to express myself and share with people and be of service all at the same time. And I highly recommend you do the same.

Let go of the fear of being "found out." Own your story. Share your stories of challenge and triumph.

And if you have several years' experience, please share it. Otherwise, you're doing everyone else a disservice by not getting out there and sharing yourself, walking through that discomfort if necessary, and contributing your knowledge and expertise. Truth is— what's on the other side of that is so much more exciting and walking through that fear pays huge dividends. Be a Mentor. Be contagious. Your passion will lead to your purpose.

10
SUCCESS IS AN INSIDE JOB

If you give a room full of EAs, any problem, any challenge —whatever it is—it is absolutely incredible to see what they can create together. Nothing's impossible. We are skilled, smart, thoughtful, resourceful, effective, proficient, determined, careful, inventive, creative, and productive. Then why is it that many of us feel under-appreciated and unfulfilled?

If I could snap my fingers and instantly give all EAs more of something, it would be confidence. I think every single one of us wonders at times, "Am I doing this right? Do they appreciate me? Do they see me? Am I valued?" Particularly when we make mistakes or when it comes to conversations about money. But first and foremost, you simply must choose to answer "Yes" to all of those questions. Confidence isn't something you earn; it's something you choose. You're working with executives. Many of you even have the word "executive" in your title. So, choose to be confident, and it will speak volumes and come across in how you show up to others. It will elicit more confidence in you from others, too. It will come full circle, and you won't have to ask yourself those questions anymore.

How you're treated is how you're perceived.
–Phoenix Normand

But here's the thing. How did I become great at what I do? (Yep, I said it!) By risking and inviting failure. I have failed, and I have made mistakes, plain and simple. But I learned that by refusing to harp on failures or to see imperfections as catastrophes, I can use those experiences as powerful learning opportunities. Think about it—did your moments of growth originate from cruising and coasting along in life? My guess is they didn't. They likely came from moments of discomfort or pain. From tough, often emotionally-charged, conversations. So, what does that mean? Failure—re-conceived—helps us grow, deepens our experience, and ultimately turns into confidence.

Winning is an inside job. Until you're winning on the inside, you can't expect to win-at least sustainably-on the outside.

One habit that can drain your confidence from the penthouse to the basement is comparing yourself to others. There's no upside—it's all downside. For the longest time, I used to compare myself to others for all sorts of reasons. I'd compare myself to people who were enrolled in all the extracurricular activities at school, those who went to camp, went skiing, or those who had siblings, fathers and highly functioning moms. I felt I didn't measure up—to whom, I'm not exactly sure—but I didn't feel worthy. Ever. I'd always come up short.

It's easy to think other people are perfect, so it's important to remember that, just like your own highlight reel, there is so much more to another person's life than what you see, hear, read, and experience in day-to-day interactions. You never know what someone's been through to get to where they are. Besides, who knows if they're happy? What matters is *you*. You have incredible gifts to share with the world. You might think, "Maggie, I'm not special, I haven't done anything…what's my unique gift?" You're not alone in thinking that way. I've been there myself.

So, I suggest that you ask yourself these questions: First, what are you most proud of or what lights you up? Then, what's something most people don't know about you? Finally, what's something that's happened to you? Or a life-changing event you've been through? Something that's scary, painful, or dark that may have impacted how you showed up and viewed the world? What if you could use your darkest moments and create your greatest gifts?

"Maggie, that's impossible—no way," I hear you saying. "Besides, I'd never want to share *that* with anyone. There's too much guilt and shame. What would people *think*?" I felt that way for a long time, too, until, one day, something shifted inside me. I figured that if I can't get comfortable with everything I've experienced, been through, and walked through—if I can't eventually share that with others so they understand they're not alone and there's so much aliveness on the other side of it all—then *what's the point*? If I hadn't reached that point of acceptance, walking through the fear and vulnerability, and eventually sharing to let others know they're not alone in their experiences, then you wouldn't be reading this. Period.

In 2019, when I was a guest on The Leader Assistant Podcast (Episode #33), hosted by Jeremy Burrows, he asked me what I was most proud of. I replied, "I can tell you that I'm proud of my insatiable curiosity. I can tell you that I'm proud of my relentless pursuit of training and development. But I would be remiss if I didn't share one more thing because it's absolutely core to who I am today. And, I know without question that I wouldn't be where I am today professionally if I'd hadn't made this decision a few years ago."

By justifying your problems, you recommit to them.
−Russell Brand

I said, "This is the first time I'm sharing this publicly, but I want to be congruent with what I share and practice authenticity in all that I say and do. So here it is: I made the decision to stop drinking about six years ago. And that's been so impactful to how I show up for myself and in life personally and professionally."

My "secret" was out, and I felt like a ton of bricks had been lifted from my shoulders. Not only that, after the episode aired, several people reached out to me on LinkedIn saying they, too, had stopped drinking. "Thank you for sharing that," they said. "That's so brave. I thought was the only one… Now I know I'm not alone." This of course further reinforced the notion that what we spend so much time and energy burying, hiding, and outright denying, could in fact have a positive impact on those around you. So, share!

People don't want to hear from a hero. They want to relate. You want to be authentic and vulnerable? Share the shit. Tell your Truth. That's what's real, raw, and resonates.

When I first got sober, my sponsor at the time told me that I was "going to get to know who Maggie is." I thought she was ridiculous and full of shit. I couldn't comprehend what she was trying to tell me by saying that. Until I did. She was right. The clouds finally cleared, and for the first time I was able to start building my confidence, discovering myself, and liking—and eventually loving—myself. I went from carrying a generalized self-loathing to feeling more acceptance and love for myself than I ever thought possible. And for that, I am most proud.

Your thoughts can be bricks on your pathway to freedom—or the bars of your prison. Your thoughts shape your beliefs, your beliefs shape your actions, your actions determine your behavior, your behaviors become your habits, and your habits dictate your life. What you believe about yourself can either limit you or invite you to expand and grow. Your thoughts have great power to influence your feelings and ultimately to determine your life experience. So, if you tend to have negative thoughts, start paying attention to what you are feeding your mind. When you have those thoughts, redirect them. If imposter syndrome starts to take hold in you as it did in me, don't let it. There are many books written on the topic, but I feel it's important to call it out here: You are not your thoughts! Do not allow those disempowering stories to hold you back from living the life you desire. Please! You are so much more than your thoughts.

We become what we think about.
−Earl Nightingale, The Strangest Secret

The Drive to Grow

It's part of our DNA. In order to feel most alive, vibrant, and fulfilled in life, we have to grow beyond who we know ourselves to be. We *must* evolve. That means we have to—no, we *get* to—learn, create, and contribute, and not just stay stagnant and stuck. I know it's true for me, and I think it's true for everyone. At some point, I realized that, while I could limit myself to doing calendaring, travel, and expenses and still get a stellar performance review, I was hungry for more. *A lot* more. I was made for more. And you are, too.

I believe hunger is one of the most important pieces of the puzzle to have as an EA. You're propelled forward if you're hungry to learn, to continuously improve, to deliver. You're lit up if you've got a hunger to find out whatever it is that you want to find out, to achieve something, to create something, or to hit whatever timeline you're looking to hit. Or even a hunger to get it right with core things like dealing with calendaring, travel, and expenses. If a hotel is sold out at the conference center, what are you going to do? Well, you're going to FITFO—because that's what you do. You always deliver because your goal is to make the life of your executive easier. The hunger and determination to figure things out, to get things done, to make it happen—all make you extraordinary in your role. And that hunger is best served when you see that your job is not about you. Again, it's about helping your executive reach their next level. Remember?

Consistency compounds, just
like money in the bank.
−John C. Maxwell

So I recommend that people feed that hunger and commit to continuous growth. You will be amazed at how much more exciting life gets and how much more alive you feel. Risking failure and imperfection and uncertainty. Reaching out beyond your comfort zones to taste newness and challenge and even success. Discover talents you don't even know you have.

The quality of your life is in direct proportion to the amount of uncertainty you can comfortably deal with.
–Tony Robbins

Every day, choose and commit to do and give 10% more of yourself than you did the day before. If that's too much, start with 1% per day. I used to think that if you do that for a whole year, you'd improve by about 3.65% by the end of the year, right? And that's pretty good! But then I realized I didn't even do the math right. Since consistency compounds, like John Maxwell says, so your return will be even more. According to Zappos, if you increase what you have by 1% each day, then at the end of the year, you have 37.78 times what you had at the beginning of the year. That's huge!

Today, when I look back over just the last few years and think about all the trainings, events, and conferences that I've been to, and it was only a few years ago when I was an EA whose brain was atrophying—or so I thought—I am blown away!

Commit to improving 1% each day and become 37 times better by the end of the year.

Whatever it is that you want to do, you can absolutely do. But the question is: who do you need to become to do it? When you think about it, what got you *here* won't get you *there*. The person that got you to this existence, this life experience, isn't going to get you to the next one—to where we want to go.

So, where does your hunger lead? What do you want to do? Write a book? Become a speaker? Get some more training? Contribute? Write blog posts? Inspire others through your work, directly and indirectly? Apply for a big job you have your eye on? Lead a team of EAs? Become a COS or even COO? Then go for it. Dream BIG. Begin the journey—*today*. Put one foot in front of the other.

Start taking action. And then continue to be in action, because it's not about checking off one check box, it's about making a commitment to a way of life, putting in the time, taking steps and making progress to get you where you want to go. And I can pretty much guarantee that you will be surprised to discover who you are when you do that.

What's *one* thing you could do *today* to actively propel you toward your dream or vision? Go do it. Make it happen.

Relentless Pursuit

As you've seen, I've invested tons of time and money on my personal and professional development in the last few years. In 2018, I completed 250+ hours in trainings and more than 450 hours in 2019. I know that's not attainable to everyone, but I feel that if I'm able to synthesize what I learn, make it my own, provide nuggets of skills and empowering perspectives, I think that's truly impactful.

Without question, I know that I am where I am today because of my relentless pursuit of training and development and my insistence on nurturing the relationships that blossomed as a result of attending those trainings. They were golden. The events themselves—finely tailored to the audiences—and the impact of their featured speakers—bringing with them incredible histories and accomplishments—can change the course of your professional trajectory. Learn from them as you attend events and *choose* to engage with them more directly for an even greater amplitude of effect. Don't just attend events and let that experience and knowledge die on the vine. Go build, create, implement, and share!

After all, if you're not growing, you're dying. So, whether or not there's a budget for learning and development at your company, decide and commit to investing in yourself and *your* future. Include training as your new normal. Risk learning something. Fully immerse yourself and watch the magic unfold. Learn. learn. learn.

Out of your deepest pain will come your greatest gifts, but it can only happen when you take control of the meaning.
–Tony Robbins

Today, I walk a fine line of balancing time-consuming knowledge and implementing it. You can consume all sorts of material and meet lots of people, but if you're not doing anything with it—sharing, teaching, creating, building, coaching, training, writing, or speaking—to name a few!—what good is it?

So get in action. Read. Write. Learn. Get out and meet people. Don't limit your existence to the current confines of your limiting beliefs and social structure. Your efforts will reward you.

Find ways you like to learn and grow. If you're a hardcore introvert, then at least read. My hotspot and Wi-Fi network name is #ReadABook. It reminds me that, while I might consume a large volume of material in the form of posts and articles online, nothing compares to the commitment and discipline required to start and complete a book. Sometimes I have seven to ten books going at a time; I've even started two in one day. A rather foolish thing to do, but so what. I'm reading. You're either shrinking or you're growing. I choose the latter.

I also recommend listening to podcasts. There's a universe of insight and information out there waiting to be heard. For several years, during my commute, I've been listening to podcasts by influencers like Jeremy Burrows, Lewis Howes, Tony Robbins, Brendon Burchard, Rachel Hollis, John Maxwell, and Oprah. I also watch LinkedIn Learning broadcasts, specifically topics on leadership, executive presence, communication, and more. It all goes in the hopper and enriches my skills and perspectives. Consistency, as I said, makes a difference. My growth, my results, and my ability to make a difference have exceeded anything I could have imagined. A commitment to continuous learning makes it so.

Each moment we have on this planet is an incredible gift. Once you get in touch with that, your lens shifts from lack, less-than, and won't happen to one of gratitude, abundance, love, and joy.

While I'm on the subject of learning, I want to stress the importance of financial literacy. Consider signing up for Mint, Betterment, and start an Acorns account. Educate yourself about money. For starters, think about paying yourself first, contributing to IRAs, 401Ks, or an individual/taxable account. Make sure you have a savings account that's separate from your checking account (Ally is a great place to start). These are the minimum steps to take to build your framework and put your investments on autopilot. There are so many options to sculpt your financial future. Don't wait until you're "ready" or out of debt, or whatever else may be holding you back. Start saving and investing today. Your future depends on it.

And you're worth it.

Now, while I recommend that you build your network, take classes, get more involved in meetings, and expand your training, I want to point out that the suggestion especially applies if you work for small to medium-sized companies, not so much the huge monoliths like Facebook and Google, where job functions are precisely defined. Within the smaller organizations, you have an opportunity (or imperative!) to wear many hats, some voluntarily and others not so much, just because there are gaps that need to be filled. At 6sense, for example, my role was never just to do calendaring, travel and expenses. Even when we were at 40 people two and a half years ago, there was so much more to do. Now that we're at 200+, the needs and requirements of my job have grown right along with the headcount. At the same time, I realized I have a say in the ways my role might expand and in considering what might be the best ways to up-level my performance.

If you're working with an executive who supports your growth, you'll have even more opportunities to expand your role the way you want to. (And if he or she doesn't support your growth, or you haven't asked for it, broach the conversation.) Even beyond inbox management and the occasional personal tasks, for example, if there's no HR infrastructure, you might contribute in that way. Help to build the company culture or even become the culture champion within the organization. You might set up meetings with the CMO or HR to talk about upcoming events or to discuss where they want the culture of the company to go. You might sit in on leadership meetings and track timelines, deliverables, and owners of specific initiatives, and then perhaps follow up with those owners because—like all of us—they're not infallible.

11
FINDING YOUR VOICE

With change comes opportunity. I was lucky enough to find out that, despite the chaos and uncertainty of a reorg, there comes an incredible opportunity to stop playing small, to up your game and discover more of your greatness. Some EAs choose to hide behind the scenes and just take direction and generally don't offer their opinion unless they get asked. And, even then, they might not share what they really think. But I think it is ultimately a costly response. It can cost you your potential, and it might also cost the team and the organization that you work for.

Opportunity comes hand in hand with your willingness to speak up and be heard. As an EA, we have incredible insight into people, processes, and the business. We have valuable perspective and experience. So, for everyone's benefit, speak up!

When a new executive is coming on board, your job is to manage change. A lot of things have to happen behind the scenes to move things forward, and your voice makes a difference. Your job is all about being the connector, because, after all, there's always room for improvement when it comes to communication from the top. Many organizations fail to provide intentional, consistent communication to the company, and the fallout hurts. They send a one-and-done email. But since not everybody processes information the same way, it's necessary to send important communications *multiple times* via email, Slack, Management teams, and All-Hands to give people ongoing announcements of what's coming and the reasoning behind it. People want to know why things are happening and why decisions are being made. It's important to navigate the water cooler conversations that inevitably happen. Because let's face it, they always happen.

So please speak up!

Our executives aren't thinking about us, yet most of the time many of us are too afraid to actually speak up or offer our opinion. But why? Nobody's going to write you up, put you on a performance plan, or worse, fire you, for sharing valuable insights. The truth is that you most likely *are* welcome to offer an opinion, to sit at the table, and to contribute.

So speak up.

> *When you get, give. When you learn, teach.*
> *–Maya Angelou*

If direct isn't your style (yet), you can ask or say things like, "I'm hearing X, but I see Y," or, "I'm seeing X, but I'm hearing Y," or, "What do you think?"

These days, one of my favorite lines is, "May I make an observation?" When I say that, they know I need their ear. Sometimes I'll send a calendar invite for a quick chat later in the afternoon or ask to go for a walk around the block. People can be fearful, especially during a reorg, feeling like they have a target on their back. So, communicate. Keep the flow open. Serve as the motivator, reminding people that with change comes opportunity.

Even beyond your interactions with your boss, try making communication your new normal. So much of the success and accomplishment I now enjoy is rooted in conversations and outreach I've made to people. Comfortably or uncomfortably, I've reached out to people, took action, tried to add value, and communicated honestly.

The results have been phenomenal because I spoke up. I now count many influencers as my mentors and friends, and I have been enriched by them a thousand-fold.

Ownership

2018 was a huge year for me and it was largely because that's when I started choosing to take 100% responsibility for my life. I was investing in myself and my future. I embraced ownership over my work, behavior, failures, and even thoughts. Never before had it occurred to me that I was 100% responsible for my life. I was so accustomed to blaming others, and focusing on what I couldn't, wouldn't, or didn't do. I was letting those excuses define my life. And when I looked back, I saw that through all the trauma, abandonment, abuse, addiction, feelings of unworthiness and more, and I had let those thoughts, feelings, and things define me, too. I lived life as though life was happening *to* me instead of *for* me.

Now I know I don't have to. I look back now, and, as much as I suffered then, I wouldn't change a thing. A lot of it wasn't easy or fun. But today I consider myself an example of what's possible when you take radical, intentional action and own your life.

Taking 100% responsibility can change everything. The moment you realize you are 100% responsible for where you are today, you can experience a life of transformation and watch the magic unfold. Let go of needing to be right. Give up making other people wrong. Apply that to how you show up in life and watch your life transform.

Taking responsibility can include ownership of your circumstances, even how others treat you. I'm a firm believer that you get what you tolerate. I run into people who feel they aren't being respected, and I ask them to look at how they are showing up in their role. Are you being respectful? Are you confident? What are you projecting? What kind of energy are you bringing into the room? How's your tone? How's your body language? How's your delivery? I absolutely recognize that there are extremely difficult people out there, but I want to invite people to think about how they're showing up in their role, too. Because your communication, whether verbal or nonverbal, can absolutely make all the difference in the interaction.

The most profound transformations can occur from the simplest realizations: You are enough. You are more than enough. You, and only you, have the power to radically alter your life. If you can do that—100%—you can soar to unimaginable heights in your lifetime.

Dream It. Write It. Create it.

It doesn't matter what it is you dream about or what you want to create, I believe that the first step to realizing it is to speak it or write it down. When you do, the winds of the universe seem to get behind you, and magic happens. I know that every time in my life that I've written down my goals, even if I really didn't think it would happen, when I went back and looked—whether it was six months, a year, or two years later—it had happened.

For two decades, I said I wanted to go to Italy in elasticized waist pants. Seriously! For the longest time, I'd say, sort of tongue-in-cheek, that I wanted to go to Italy in elasticized waist pants—meaning I could eat my way through the country and not worry about it. And I wrote it down. And then, in September 2018, there I was, sitting on a plane bound for Italy, and it all came flooding back to me. "I'm flying to Italy in my yoga pants!" Wow! The power of the spoken word.

Watch your thoughts, they become words; watch your words, they become actions; watch your actions, they become habits; watch your habits, they become character; watch your character, for it becomes your destiny.
–Lao Tzu

A few years ago, I got a taste of the power of words when I was working with a fairly evolved CEO who liked to engage her employees. During the holidays, she made a practice of having all of us do a writing exercise. She told us to come up with two lists and write them on those large white flipchart sheets people use in presentations: first, what we're grateful for and second, what our goals are for the following year. But instead of writing, "I want this" or "I'm going to have, be, or do that," she instructed us to write everything down in the present tense, as if it's so right now. So I wrote my list of goals:

putting 20% of my income into savings; be in the best shape of my life; going to yoga five times a week; having a happy, healthy relationship with my husband; being committed to lifelong learning; having a harmonious relationship with my boss (this was before I worked with Jason). I wrote down nine things, none of which were true for me at the time. I thought it was a silly exercise, and just for fun, I stuck it in the back of my closet when I got home. But a year and a half later, I was standing in my closet and the list, usually hiding behind other things, caught my eye. And I was in shock. *OMG*! I thought. I go to yoga five days a week. Check! I put away 20% of my income to my savings. Check! I *am* in the best shape of my life. Check! And I went through the entire list of nine things and I realized that I hit every single one of them. I was incredulous!

They say that when you write down what you want, two important things happen. First, the writing itself creates new neuropathways in your brain, and second, the writing tells your brain to go get it. I believe it's because I wrote it all down that it happened. I've continued to write things down and I notice results. I believe that my connection with Al-Husein Madhany flourished because I wrote down what I envisioned with him, yet I had no idea how things would play out initially. So, write your dreams and desires down! They just might come true.

Useful Tidbits

I have just a few more tips and tricks to share with you—habits that I get a lot of benefit from—that will also hopefully make your life as an EA more successful, more fulfilling, and more rewarding. Ready?

Focus on outcomes. Instead of thinking, "I need to do A, I need to do B, I need to do C," consider what is the outcome you're going for. If you want to launch a philanthropic effort, what are the results you're aiming for? Instead of focusing on the steps in front of you, keep the goal in mind. Instead of just listing and getting bogged down with menial tasks that make up the process, think about what you are actually trying to achieve. In your EA role, what's your desired outcome for the year? For the month? For the week? How are you adding value? How are you contributing? Keep the end in mind.

Make decision-making easier. At the end of the day, our execs are human beings, and they, too, get overwhelmed with decision fatigue. So, when I have a bunch of questions to ask my executive, I will list the basic options for them to choose from. And I won't just say, "Do you want to go with pink or blue?" I'll say, "Hey, here's pink. Here's why I think we should do this. Here's where I don't think we should do this and the concerns. And here's blue. Here's why this is a better recommendation. What would you like to do?" And when I present it that way, if I've done my research, and the rapport is there, they'll generally go with my recommendation. They know that I've put in the time and the energy so they don't have to. And I've made their decision-making that much more smooth, effective, and efficient.

Let go of the need to be right. This is one of my favorite things I've learned in my trainings. Any time anyone came up to me to say something, I used to feel like I was being put on the defensive, having to explain myself. On the positive side, because of it, I was passionate about doing my research before presenting ideas or facts— to minimize the risk that I'd be caught off guard or unprepared. So, I'd be right a lot, but not always, of course. But the need to be right is a killer and ultimately telegraphs your insecurity to everyone, defeating the purpose. After all, do you really need to score that point? Do you need to feel good about yourself at someone else's expense? Letting go of that need removes barriers to relationships and opens doors to learning more. It opens the door to real connection—human to human.

Besides getting into the habit of blaming and gossiping, it's easy to fall into the trap of needing to make other people wrong—which is the flip side of needing to be right. But it's still finger-pointing. "You didn't do that right. Here's why you're wrong. So-and-So didn't do XYZ. You didn't get this to me in time, so I couldn't do that." It's just making other people look bad in hopes of making yourself look good. Instead, give yourself permission to develop a sense of curiosity. Ask questions instead of explaining or defending.

Even with my husband, I've made the mistake of needing to be right (All. Day. Long.) We'd be loading the dishwasher, and I'd make a stink about him not putting the forks facing down the "right" way. But who really cares about such things? In the grand scheme of things, it's less about being right and more about maintaining the health and integrity of the relationship—whether personal or professional.

Build punch lists. You have a finite amount of time to interact with your executive, whether it's over the phone, via text message, or on email. And so instead of asking, "Hey, did you get that communication, or did you get that other thing?" I like to maintain a punch list. Any time he calls, he gets the punch list. Even if I can squeeze in only one question off of "The List" because I don't know when I'll hear from him next, and I'm certainly not going to wait for our weekly 1:1 to move things along. (And he's learned to avoid calling unless he's ready for a punch list!) But I don't just send him one-off emails, either. I aggregate everything and then I go through it when I know there's an available time for him. I also keep in mind if it's early in the morning or late at night and adapt to his work style and timeline. We've saved tons of time on both ends this way.

I'd worked with another executive who was, you could say, "not at their best" at 2 p.m. in the afternoon. (Coffee, anyone?) This was great information as I avoided scheduling important meetings during that time, but it was prime real estate for reviewing The List. So, watch, listen, and absorb—their behaviors will likely show you more than they'll ever tell you. Become an expert at pattern recognition.

Be your best you. While success is an inside job, how you show up in the world can influence how people treat you, respond to you, and listen to you. How are you showing up to your role? What's your body language? What's your tone of voice? Your delivery? Consider how you're presenting yourself to the world and make adjustments. It might sound simple-minded, but it pays to stand up straight, speak slowly, and listen with the intent to understand instead of being understood. Give one-word answers where appropriate instead of a meadow report. Less is more; it usually indicates confidence in your abilities. When you have a less than pleasant interaction with someone, do your best to respond with empathy and compassion—the prickly people need it most.

Remember that, at our core, our role is about making things possible for others. We're here to serve, to be of service, to be a contribution instead of a hindrance. Our role is to anticipate and ensure our colleagues have what they need to function at a higher level, which enables their teams, and ultimately the company, to succeed. It's a valuable service so show up for it at your best.

Seek to be of service. In my mind, being of service is the ultimate reward. My husband and I often ask each other, "What are you grateful for?" and he laughs at me because I like to respond with, "Everything!" Because my life is full. I know that I contribute and add value to other people's lives. I'm of service; I make a difference; I make an impact. And I'm incredibly grateful to be a part of the change that I want to see.

> *I am of the opinion that my life belongs to the whole community, and as long as I live it, is my privilege to do for it whatever I can.*
> *–George Bernard Shaw*

***

Bottom line? The ultimate outcome is living your own elevated paradigm shift. Sometimes I get so caught up in the day-to-day details that I miss the miracle of what I've achieved. Somewhere through the process of radical, intentional action, I went from victim to voracious learner to finding my voice and using it to articulate my role as an executive assistant. I went from doing tasks that might be considered reactive and low on the spectrum of autonomy to being proactive about my own growth and development. And now I enjoy the freedom, flexibility, and autonomy of a position that I am helping to define, expand, and make more and more meaningful.

I invite you to step into your own greatness, too. Dream BIG. Relentlessly pursue your goals. Commit to self-investment. Speak up for yourself. Establish boundaries. Add value. Be of greater service than you ever imagined—and discover your own elevated self.

*I want to be thoroughly used up when I die,
for the harder I work the more I live. I rejoice in life
for its own sake. Life is no "brief candle" for me. It is
a sort of splendid torch which I have got hold of for
the moment, and I want to make it burn as brightly
as possible before handing it on to
future generations.*

–George Bernard Shaw

AUTHOR'S POINTS OF CONTACT

Maggie Jacobs

🌐 maggiejacobs.com

📷 @magstir

🐦 @maggiejacobs_

f @TheElevatedEA

in linkedin.com/in/maggiejacobs

Made in the USA
Las Vegas, NV
27 March 2021

20271602R00083